D0867128

Corporations and the Public Interest

CORPORATIONS AND THE PUBLIC INTEREST

GUIDING THE INVISIBLE HAND

Steven Lydenberg

BERRETT-KOEHLER PUBLISHERS, INC.
San Francisco

HD
60
.L96
2005

COPYRIGHT © 2005 BY STEVEN LYDENBERG
All rights reserved. No part of this publication may be reproduced, distributed, or transmitted in any form or by any means, including photocopying, recording, or other electronic or mechanical methods, without the prior written permission of the publisher, except in the case of brief quotations embodied in critical reviews and certain other noncommercial uses permitted by copyright law. For permission requests, write to the publisher, addressed "Attention: Permissions Coordinator," at the address below.

BERRETT-KOEHLER PUBLISHERS, INC.
235 Montgomery Street, Suite 650
San Francisco, California 94104-2916
Tel: (415) 288-0260   Fax: (415) 362-2512   www.bkconnection.com

ORDERING INFORMATION
Quantity sales. Special discounts are available on quantity purchases by corporations, associations, and others. For details, contact the "Special Sales Department" at the Berrett-Koehler address above.
Individual sales. Berrett-Koehler publications are available through most bookstores. They can also be ordered directly from Berrett-Koehler: Tel: (800) 929-2929; Fax: (802) 864-7626; www.bkconnection.com.
Orders for college textbook/course adoption use. Please contact Berrett-Koehler: Tel: (800) 929-2929; Fax: (802) 864-7626.
Orders by U.S. trade bookstores and wholesalers. Please contact Publishers Group West, 1700 Fourth Street, Berkeley, California 94710. Tel: (510) 528-1444; Fax (510) 528-3444.

Berrett-Koehler and the BK logo are registered trademarks of Berrett-Koehler Publishers, Inc.

PRINTED IN THE UNITED STATES OF AMERICA

Berrett-Koehler books are printed on long-lasting acid-free paper. When it is available, we choose paper that has been manufactured by environmentally responsible processes. These may include using trees grown in sustainable forests, incorporating recycled paper, minimizing chlorine in bleaching, or recycling the energy produced at the paper mill.

LIBRARY OF CONGRESS CATALOGING-IN-PUBLICATION DATA
Lydenberg, Steven D.
    Corporations and the public interest : guiding the invisible hand / by Steven Lydenberg.
        p. cm.
    Includes bibliographical references and index.
    ISBN-13: 978-1-57675-291-3
    1. Social responsibility of business. 2. Corporations—Moral and ethical aspects. 3. Investments—Moral and ethical aspects. I. Title.
        HD60.L96 2004
        658.4'08—dc22   2004057111

FIRST EDITION
10 09 08 07 06 05   10 9 8 7 6 5 4 3 2 1

Copyediting: Sandra Beriss. Interior design: Richard Wilson. Indexing: Rachel Rice/ Content Directions. Proofreading: Susan Seefelt Lesieutre.

The text of this book was set in Verdigris from MvB Type and Trade Gothic from Adobe.

TO ROBIN

Contents

Preface

THIS BOOK HAS GROWN FROM MY ONGOING EFFORTS TO UNDER-
stand how the field of socially responsible investing, in which I have
worked for nearly thirty years, and the related field of corporate social
responsibility, which has emerged from obscurity to considerable
prominence over this time, can contribute to the debate that is raging
today about the proper role of corporations in society. Or to put it differently, how can these two fields fulfill their promise to help direct corporations to the public interest?

In 1975 when I began my career, the joke about corporate social
responsibility was that it was an oxymoron, a contradiction in terms.
When I explained what I was doing to others, they laughed knowingly
and shook their heads. Since then, however, socially responsible investing (SRI) and corporate social responsibility (CSR) have gained a prominence and acceptance that I find difficult to comprehend.

The practice of socially responsible investing has spread around
the world, where it is known variously as ethical investing, sustainable
investing, triple-bottom-line investing, and best-of-class investing.
Corporate social responsibility has been adopted internationally,
encompassing such concepts as corporate social performance, corporate citizenship, stakeholder management, and corporate community
involvement.[1]

I have been surprised by these developments because I never
expected these fields to be more than a sideline in the worlds of finance
and corporate management. I have been encouraged because I see the

work of many over the past three decades paying off. But I also worry about the ability of these two movements to live up to the expectations they have created.

The broad outlines of SRI were established in the early 1970s, when the first socially screened mutual funds were established. These included the Pax World Funds, founded by Luther Tyson and Jack Corbett (along with Anthony and Paul Brown), and the Dreyfus Premier Third Century Fund, which both still figure prominently today. Under the leadership of Timothy Smith, the Interfaith Center on Corporate Responsibility was coordinating the filing of church-sponsored shareholder resolutions urging corporations to take society's concerns more to heart. Under Alice Tepper Marlin's direction, the Council on Economic Priorities, where I started to work in 1975, was publishing the first rankings of the social and environmental performance of U.S. companies in the pulp and paper, electric utility, banking, and military contracting industries. Pioneers such as Chuck Matthei at the Institute for Community Economics (ICE) and Mary Houghton, Milton Davis, James Fletcher, and Ronald Grzywinski at South Shore Bank (now ShoreBank) in Chicago were showing how investments at the community level could bring about meaningful societal change. These were untested initiatives, viewed as oddities, and unacknowledged by the mainstream—or if acknowledged, seen only as something to be discredited or dismissed.

In the late 1970s and early 1980s, the SRI field begin to expand. Franklin Research and Development Corporation (now Trillium Asset Management Corporation), led by Joan Bavaria, became the first money management firm devoted exclusively to these types of investments. United States Trust Company of Boston became the first mainstream bank to establish an in-house SRI team, led by SRI pioneer Robert Zevin. (This unit is now called Walden Asset Management, and the bank is known as Boston Trust & Investment Management Company.) Working Assets, founded by Jerry Dodson and John Harrington and five other early leaders, launched one of the first SRI money market funds and later pioneered the concept of affinity credit cards and long-distance phone services that donated a portion of revenues to progressive charitable causes. Also at that time, the Calvert Group began to build its family of socially screened mutual funds.

During the latter half of the 1980s, major pension funds in the United States and abroad took part in the South Africa divestment movement, refusing to invest in certain companies operating under that country's apartheid regime and establishing SRI screening as a broadly accepted tactic—and market—for the first time. The idea that consumers might take information on companies' social and environmental records into account in their shopping decisions was introduced by the Council on Economic Priorities (CEP) in 1986. I coauthored CEP's *Rating America's Corporate Conscience*, which provided consumers in the shopping aisles with ratings of companies' social and environmental records.[2] This book was followed over the next decade with CEP's *Shopping for a Better World* series.

During those years I became interested in the use of this data in the financial world. I joined Franklin Research in 1987 in order to learn more about SRI and its relationship to mainstream investing. There I watched as Joan Bavaria launched the CERES Principles with Denis Hayes. These were a set of environmental principles for corporations that were inspired in part by the *Exxon Valdez* oil spill in Alaska. These principles, in turn, served as the basis for the groundbreaking work of the CERES organization under the leadership of Robert Massie, Jr., and Mindy Lubber, and as precursors to the guidelines developed by the Global Reporting Initiative. During that time I also saw the establishment of the Social Investment Forum, the trade association of the SRI world in the United States, and the emergence of SRI in the United Kingdom, notably through the creation of funds by the Quaker-affiliated insurance company Friends Provident (now part of ISIS Asset Management).

In the 1990s I joined with Amy Domini and Peter Kinder to found Kinder, Lydenberg, Domini & Co., now KLD Research & Analytics, the first research firm devoted to marketing comprehensive social and environmental data on publicly traded companies to the financial community. Working out of two rooms in the back of an old Victorian house in Cambridge, Massachusetts, we gambled that there was a market for this research and for the SRI funds we were developing. To help spur the growth of these markets and reduce the barriers to social investing (one of KLD's core missions), we edited *The Social Investment Almanac* and coauthored *Investing for Good*, two books that surveyed the state of the field at that time.[3] During those years I was still unsure whether SRI was a viable movement that would survive, particularly when the much-desired dismantling of apartheid in South Africa came about in the early 1990s, because the protests over apartheid had been so closely associated with SRI.

As it turned out, the mid-1990s brought a domestic and international explosion of interest in both SRI and CSR. In the United States, assets under SRI management went from $1.18 trillion in 1997 to $2.32 trillion in 2001.[4] Shareholder resolutions on social and environmental issues gained increasing support despite management opposition.[5] ShoreBank became a model for a growing number of community development banks and credit unions around the country, as did ICE for community development loan funds.

During the 1990s, corporate social responsibility also established itself in the corporate community as a concept that managers around the world needed to contend with. Although not all of them embraced its principles in their handling of employee relations, community affairs, customer satisfaction, and the environment, CSR initiatives began to flourish at numerous firms. Business for Social

Responsibility, an association of U.S. corporations devoted to promoting CSR best practices, was established and eventually thrived. CSR
became an established academic discipline, advanced through the work
of theoreticians associated with groups such as the International Association for Business and Society. The concept of social entrepreneurship took hold, encouraging the nonprofit world to adopt for-profit
tactics to further their goals and the corporate world to tackle the social
in their daily business.[6]

During that decade, SRI and CSR began to take hold around the
world. In Canada, Michael Jantzi Research Associates led the development of SRI research. In Asia, the efforts of Tessa Tennant at ASrIA in
Hong Kong, Mitzue Tsukushi at the Good Bankers Co. in Japan, and
others broke new ground. In Bangladesh, Muhammad Yunus of
Grameen Bank worked to establish microlending—that is, making
small loans to individual entrepreneurs, primarily women—as a model
that soon took hold in developing countries around the world. In Brus-
sels, the European Union increasingly made CSR a part of the social
agenda for its member states. In the United Kingdom, the government
made CSR a responsibility at the ministerial level. The French required
corporations to report extensive social and environmental data in their
annual reports to shareholders. The Swedish government mandated
that the seven national multi-billion-dollar pension funds adopt some
ethical or corporate governance guidelines in their investment policies.[7]
Most recently, in 2004, the primary French state pension fund began to
apply sustainable investment criteria to a portion of its assets valued at
approximately $3.6 billion.[8] In May 2004, South Africa's Johannesburg
Securities Exchange (JSE) launched the JSE Socially Responsible
Investment Index, which included fifty-one companies listed on the
exchange that met the index's sustainability requirements.[9] Meanwhile,
the first Global Compact Leaders Summit was held in June 2004 at
U.N. headquarters in New York. The United Nations had established its

xiv   Preface

Global Compact, through which business endorsers agree to consider ten fundamental principles in their conduct, in 1999. As of September 2004, the Global Compact had over seventeen hundred participants.[10]

Perhaps I shouldn't have been surprised by these developments, but I was. I asked myself why interest in SRI and CSR was now springing up throughout the world. Was what we were doing in the 1990s so different from our work of the two previous decades? Why were governments, particularly in Europe, promoting CSR so vigorously? What did the public or governments expect these two fields to offer? Many of us who had long pursued SRI and CSR were interested in genuine change, but what about the others? Were the critics of corporations and globalization correct when they asserted that CSR and SRI were only being taken up by the corporate world to make a power grab more palatable? Could investors and consumers committed to SRI and CSR really play an effective role in directing hardheaded management of corporations to public ends?

When I looked around the worlds of SRI and CSR at that time, I saw what seemed to be a collection of anecdotal efforts and disconnected SRI and CSR claims, rather than a consistent system with an overarching view. In a first attempt to articulate a vision for SRI, I wrote an article in 2002 for the *Journal of Corporate Citizenship:* "Envisioning Socially Responsible Investing: A Model for 2006" sketched out the changes I thought were needed for a system to emerge. I soon realized, however, that I had neglected important issues about the role of government, so in a second piece appearing in autumn 2003, "Trust Building and Trust Busting: Corporations, Government, and Responsibilities," I briefly raised these larger issues.[11] But it was clear to me that both articles only scratched the surface in addressing the difficult questions of systematic and effective control. It was my continuing struggle to address these questions—to understand how SRI and CSR can act effectively in today's world and interact appropriately with government and other elements of society in their dealings with corporations—that led to the present volume.

Today, the number of new efforts under way and the speed at which they are being initiated in the fields of SRI and CSR is truly impressive. In trying to capture the spirit of the times, I profile here a number of organizations and their activities and describe a number of developments as they are unfolding. In fact, so many companies and organizations are now working in these fields that it is impossible to mention them all, and it was with great reluctance that I omitted many worthy groups and undertakings here. In addition, events are unfolding with such rapidity that I must resign myself to the fact that parts of this book will have fallen behind the times as soon as it appears in print. My goal, however, is to portray the essentials of the current situation and give an idea of where things appear to be heading. In so doing, I hope that a clearer vision of what is at stake will emerge and help steer both corporations and society to a better future.

Acknowledgments

I have had the privilege of working with many of the pioneers of the socially responsible investing world over the past three decades. They have contributed to my personal development and professional education in more ways than I can name and continue to inspire me; for all of this I owe them a debt of gratitude. In my years with the Council on Economic Priorities, with Trillium Asset Management, and KLD Research & Analytics, I had the pleasure of working with many dedicated individuals, all of whom I would like to thank for sharing with me the ups and downs of building a new field. The efforts of the Social Investment Forum and the First Affirmative Financial Network in sustaining the socially responsible investment movement over the years have given me much to be grateful for, and lifted my spirits as well. Finally, I would like to thank Amy Domini and my current colleagues at

Domini Social Investments, who have done so much to nurture this field and to sustain my own efforts in it. Their support and understanding are extraordinary and deeply appreciated.

I received many helpful comments and suggestions on drafts of this book. In particular, I would like to thank Catherine Brock, Charlie Dorris, Sylvana Habdank-Kolaczkowska, Kyle Johnson, Adam Kanzer, Elka Karl, Marjorie Kelly, Marcy Murninghan, Ted Nace, Karen Paul, Russell Sparkes, Sandra Waddock, and Allen White for their careful readings and detailed suggestions. I would also like to thank Steve Piersanti and Jeevan Sivasubramaniam of Berrett-Koehler Publishers for their invaluable editorial suggestions and conceptual guidance throughout the manuscript's development, and Sandra Beriss for her perceptive and thorough copyediting. David Wood proved to be not only a terrific research assistant but a much-needed provider of feedback on the focus and direction of the book as it evolved.

In the interests of full disclosure, I want to note that I have an ownership position in two of the organizations described in this book—KLD Research & Analytics and Domini Social Investments—and that Domini Social Investments has submanagement contracts for two of its funds with ShoreBank, which is profiled here as well. However, the opinions and representations in this book are mine alone, and not those of Domini Social Investments, KLD Research & Analytics, or any other organization.

Last but not least, I would like to express my gratitude and love to my wife, Robin, and my daughter, Annica, for their support not only for this project but for so many things over the years.

Steven Lydenberg
Brookline, Massachusetts
August 2004

Introduction

AT THE HEART OF THIS BOOK IS A SERIES OF RECOMMENDATIONS about what can be done to create practical tools for investors, consumers, corporate managers, employees, regulators, and legislators to direct corporations toward the public interest. As governments around the world have cut back their ownership and regulation of business over the past three decades and increasingly relied on markets and private enterprise, the risks of corporate abuse have been heightened and new tools are needed to manage these risks.

Under the right circumstances, marketplace forces can help direct corporations to the public interest. Ensuring that those circumstances are in place, however, is crucial. In particular, there must be widespread availability of data on corporations' social and environmental records, analysis and debate about the significance of that data, and the mechanisms to allow the marketplace to reward and punish corporations appropriately when they succeed or fail in achieving societal purposes. Creating a system that can effectively accomplish these goals will take a concerted effort by government, investors, consumers, and corporations themselves.

Steering business toward wealth creation and societal benefit is a goal shared both by those who advocate market-based approaches—despite the risks of abuse and social disruption—and by those who advocate governmental control and regulation—despite the risks of waste, corruption, and stultification. Differing approaches to achieving this end have provoked political controversy over the past century.

Many of the proposals I make in this book lie at the point where these differing approaches intersect.

The book is divided into two parts, the first dealing with theory and context and the second with practical implications. In part 1, I explain why concern about corporations and the public interest has grown recently, what public interest corporations can reasonably be expected to serve, and the general strategies taken to date by the socially responsible investing (SRI) and corporate social responsibility (CSR) movements to steer corporations toward those interests. In part 2, I focus on specific steps that will need to be taken to enable investors and consumers to influence corporate behavior, including those best taken by government.

Chapter 1 reminds readers of the tremendous shift away from government and toward markets that has occurred over the past three decades, including privatization, deregulation, and for-profit corporations providing services traditionally seen as the responsibility of the public sphere. Those advocating this shift have promised a richer, better world, but a surge in corporate scandals, financial crises, power struggles between government and business, and displays of management greed, along with daily reminders of widespread poverty and despair, have given critics powerful arguments for government oversight and control. The chapter also provides some historical context on the ongoing power struggle between government and business that has played out since the eighteenth century.

As corporations have gained power and influence while governments have trimmed back, the expectations that corporations will act in the public interest have increased. But there is a dilemma: How can government-like controls guide corporations to the public interest in an era when government is cutting back and markets are gaining greater sway? Chapter 2 begins by describing the public interest that corporations can serve. This public interest is the creation of societal value that can survive the corporation itself—what I call *long-term wealth*. Corporations create long-term wealth when, in addition to generating productivity gains, they preserve natural resources for future generations, create value in their relationships with their stakeholders, and do not externalize costs onto society. This concept is of increasing importance as the world begins a new century in which it will have a population that tests the earth's carrying capacity; transportation and communication systems that increase business's ability to efficiently and rapidly produce either profits or harm; and challenges that are global in scope that threaten the survival of the environmental, financial, and social networks of support on which we depend.

Chapter 3, the last chapter of part 1, reviews three strategies used by the SRI and CSR movements to steer companies toward the public good: *the business case* demonstrates to corporate managers where productivity and profitability coincide with the public interest; *values-driven approaches* direct those in the business world toward ethical behavior; and a *system of measurement of long-term wealth* creates indicators of corporations' ability to act in the public interest, allowing rewards to be assigned to those that succeed in doing so.

Although each approach has its strengths and limitations, a combination of all three will certainly be needed to take maximum advantage of their respective strengths and to compensate for their weaknesses. In this book, however, I focus primarily on the third approach because I believe it takes greatest advantage of the marketplace's ability to act in a new role as an *invisible hand*, one that guides corporations toward today's new conception of the public interest. To function effectively, however, this marketplace requires substantial commitments of time and resources by government and corporations and of effort by investors, consumers, and others in society. It also requires data, debate, and consequences.

Part 2 describes the progress made to date in transforming the current marketplace in ways that create this new system and envisions the next steps necessary for its full realization. Chapter 4 explains that social and environmental data on corporations' actual social and environmental records is key to the measurement of company performance. A handful of SRI research firms have already begun to identify and compile such data. Now the challenge is to ensure that corporations systematically disclose this information. Four systems of disclosure will ultimately be needed: international voluntary disclosure of company-wide data; nationally mandated disclosure of company-wide data; nationally mandated reporting of specific disaggregated data; and voluntary customized company reporting.

Chapter 5 examines what will be necessary to analyze and evaluate the data, and the open debate that will be needed to ensure a consensus on the wealth-creating potential of these corporations' initiatives. Two types of research organizations will be needed: those that process the raw data into usable formats, or what I call "infomediaries," and those that are experienced in using this processed data to compare the performance of corporations to each other—a class of organizations that I call "rating agencies."

Data collection and analysis will provide the basis for a broader, informed societal discussion on how companies relate to their employees, customers, communities, regulators, and the environment. To be effective, this debate needs to be based on widely disseminated data. It also needs to pierce the veil of technical vocabulary in which the financial and business worlds all too often have cloaked their activities. Debate will also help investors and consumers look to new ways of thinking about the fundamental concepts of price in the market, returns in investing, and corporations as citizens.

Chapter 6 looks at what it will take to create the consequences—that is, rewards and punishments. Without consequences, the data and debate will be meaningless. This crucial area is the least developed. However, some investors and consumers are defining a vision of societal wealth and communicating it to corporate management through what I call *targeted engagement, reallocation of assets,* and *broad public discourse.* These activities will need to grow and expand. To create systems that encourage such activities and allow the financial and consumer markets to send consistent signals to corporate management on these issues, government will need to take some critical steps to empower investors, consumers, and other stakeholders in the corporation.

Chapter 7 sketches out the steps that government and others might take to realize the creation of these systems and reminds the reader of the urgency of the task at hand.

By providing a broad view of the current relationship between corporations and society, I hope this book will contribute to the creation of a system that manages the challenges of the twenty-first century effectively. By mid-century, a technologically sophisticated world of nine billion people will have the potential to create tremendous good, but equal potential to create harm. Decisions made today about the relationships between corporations and society will have a crucial bearing on how successfully this potential is managed in the decades to come.

PART ONE

In Whose Interest? The Markets, Government, and the Public

CHAPTER ONE

The Current Dilemma

ONE OF THE MOST IMPORTANT QUESTIONS OF OUR TIME IS whether corporations are acting—or even whether they can act—in the public interest. This is not a new question, but it has taken on increasing urgency over the past three decades. During this time, assets and power around the world have shifted from governments to the private sector on a tremendous scale, and with this shift has come the expectation of great benefits to society. But simultaneously, business scandals, financial meltdowns, global environmental and health care crises, and persistent poverty have cast doubt on business's ability to deliver on its promises in meaningful ways. It can legitimately be asked: Are corporations really serving a public good, or are they robbing the public blind?

To answer this question, it is necessary first to resolve a dilemma that has grown out of this power shift: *How can government assure control of corporate abuse and promote the public interest without returning to the heavy hand of ownership and regulation that it has so recently turned away from?* This dilemma is a difficult one, and in my view, resolving it will require a concerted effort by government, investors, consumers, employees, and corporations themselves to create marketlike mechanisms that can guide corporations toward the public good. Markets already steer business toward the goods of productivity and innovation. But new market mechanisms—based on ample data and objective analysis, and leading to substantial consequences—must be created to successfully direct corporations to the generation of what I call *long-term wealth*.

The public's ambivalence about corporations today is palpable. Whether corporations are heartless, sociopathic machines driven to seek profit at any price or engines of wealth generation that can feed, clothe, care for, and employ today's burgeoning population is a question that provokes ongoing debate. This debate has taken on increasing urgency in the face of the wave of privatization, deregulation, experimentation with the use of markets for social services, and dismantling of trade barriers that has occurred since the late 1970s.

The extent of these reforms and the heights to which they raised hopes cannot be ignored. In the early 1990s, in the wake of the dissolution of the Soviet Union, Russia and other Eastern-bloc countries transferred assets on a monumental scale to private hands, holding out the promise of relaxed economies and more democratic political systems. In Southeast Asia, deregulation of industry and the financial markets led to seemingly miraculous growth in the economies of the "tiger" nations of the region: Thailand, Malaysia, Indonesia, and South Korea. In China, the integration of profit principles into the state-controlled economy unleashed tremendous potential for production and consumption. In Latin America and Africa, nations dismantled trade barriers and adopted stringent controls on government spending in the hopes of making rapid strides to end poverty. Meanwhile, in the United States, the federal government deregulated industry after industry—trucking, natural gas distribution, natural gas pipelines, airlines, financial services, telecommunications, media, and electric utilities—with the promise of great benefits to consumers and the economy alike.

But the political, financial, and environmental crises and criticisms that followed these reforms cannot be dismissed either. The "oligarchs" of Russia grabbed formerly state-owned assets at great personal gain and grappled for power with the government while prospects for Western-style democracy began to fade. A 1997 monetary crisis in Thailand spread by contagion across Southeast Asia to other regions of the global economy, undoing much of the economic progress all had made in a financial downturn that lasted for years. A booming Chinese economy won jobs from the developed and developing worlds alike, prompting outcries over outsourcing and worries over the loss of national industries. At the same time, China's growing consumption of energy and resources raised the specter of widespread pollution and environmental degradation. Meanwhile, a growing number of Latin American governments questioned the wisdom of the privatizations and resulting losses that neoliberal economic strategies imposed on them, and despite scattered successes, many African nations fell further into poverty. And a series of front-page accounting scandals and business frauds among the likes of Enron Corp., WorldCom (now MCI), Tyco International, HealthSouth Corporation, and Rite Aid Corporation in the United States, as well as Parmalat in Europe, raised the question that if corporations do not even deal honestly with their stockowners, how can they be trusted to serve broader societal interests?

As these historic events unfolded, I struggled to understand their significance. Because of my involvement in socially responsible investing (SRI) and corporate social responsibility (CSR) over the years, I wanted to understand the relationship between these events and the growing interest in these fields. A look back at the history of the corporation over the past three centuries helped me arrive at a number of insights into the current debates about the proper role of corporations in society and how SRI and CSR might help shape that role.[1]

The Corporation's Historical Purpose

Society has historically licensed publicly traded corporations to operate because it believes that they serve the public interest. The nature of that public interest, however, has changed over time. The largest, best-known corporations of the seventeenth and eighteenth centuries were created by charter of European governments to exploit the riches of their colonies. The most successful and long-lived of them was the British East India Company. First chartered in 1600 and not disbanded until 1874, it functioned for many years as the effective government of India. At times it was even granted the power to declare and wage war.[2] Such corporations served what was perceived as the public interest of that time—that is, exploiting the colonies—but the granting of similar privileges today is virtually inconceivable. Today's definition of how corporations can best serve the public interest is different from yesterday's, just as tomorrow's definition will be different from today's.

The struggles of governments to control potential abuse of the public interest by publicly traded corporations also date back to the eighteenth century. At one pivotal moment in 1720, two major financial scandals prompted England, France, and other European countries to impose severe restrictions on the creation of publicly traded companies; these restrictions lasted well into the nineteenth century. The two scandals resulted from the collapse of the inflated stock of England's South Sea Company and France's Mississippi Company, two companies ostensibly set up to profit from trade in the colonial world but in fact engaged primarily in speculative machinations. When these "bubbles" burst, they produced spectacular bankruptcies that threw the finances of the two nations into crisis and prompted a backlash against the concept of financing corporations through the public sale of stock.

It is also important to note that the form of the corporation that we know in modern times was created in the nineteenth century to solve one problem, but as a result, wound up creating others. The emergence of the industrial society in the mid- and late 1800s called for the construction of major infrastructures to allow the development of the railroad and telegraph systems, the exploitation of such natural resources as iron and petroleum, and the harnessing of steam-driven technology to facilitate mass production. The companies of the day were not set up to aggregate the huge amounts of capital necessary for the investments with the long payback periods that these projects required. To address this challenge, four existing legal business structures were allowed to be combined into a single entity: corporations were permitted infinite life, they were allowed to incorporate for unspecified purposes, investors' liabilities were limited to the total of their investments, and capital could be raised through publicly traded, joint ownership. The corporate structure that now dominates the business world possesses these four characteristics.

Controlling this powerful new model, the excesses it is capable of, and the political and social disruptions it is prone to cause, has challenged governments since its creation. The twentieth century through the 1970s tells the story of controls clamped on these corporations to deal with their booms and busts, their abuses, and their disruptive tendencies. At one extreme, the Russian and Chinese governments expropriated all private assets and turned the running of corporations over to the state in the name of the public interest. At the other end of the spectrum, the U.S. government created an elaborate network of regulatory agencies as waves of reform followed crises or scandals in the 1900s, the 1930s, and the 1960s and 1970s. Falling between these two approaches, European and Japanese governments gained selective or partial ownership in the corporate and financial worlds and created interlocking structures to maintain substantial control of corporate enterprises.

It is particularly instructive to note how the unemployment, labor unrest, and disparities between the rich and poor created by the markets and their regular cycles of boom and bust were seen to contribute to the great wars of the early twentieth century. For example, the liberal economist John Maynard Keynes spoke for many when he observed: "The outstanding faults of the economic society in which we live are its failure to provide for full employment and its arbitrary and inequitable distribution of wealth and incomes."[3] In an effort to achieve lasting peace after World War I, the International Labor Organization was created, along with the League of Nations, in part to ameliorate troublesome labor relations. After World War II, the multilateral financial institutions—the International Monetary Fund, the World Bank, and the General Agreement on Tariffs and Trade (now the World Trade Organization), which were created along with the United Nations—were intended in part to bind the interests of countries together through trade, while national governments were encouraged to provide full employment and social security.[4]

Today's Dilemma

I came away from this historical review understanding that the shift from government ownership and control toward market economies that was set in motion by the United Kingdom, the United States, and Russia in the 1980s and 1990s was in fact a major reversal of an almost century-long trend to control corporations. Yet there is good reason to believe that the danger of social disruption, which these controls were originally imposed to deal with, is still real.

In today's world, the cautionary tales of the past are not lost on those protesting in the streets at the meetings of the World Trade Organization in Seattle in 1999 or the G-8 summit in Genoa in 2001. They see that, if left unregulated and unmonitored, businesses can create a harsh dichotomy, something that journalist William Greider has described as "two different ethical systems [society's and capitalism's], each one with its own distinctive logic and moral code, each pursuing self-interested goals and operating premises, each one contesting for primacy in our thoughts and actions."[5] Deregulation and setting markets free often lead to manias such as the dot-com bubble of the 1990s and abuses such as those of Enron and WorldCom. At such times, even market advocates recognize the need for restraints. As one *Wall Street Journal* reporter put it recently, "Markets are a great way to organize economic activity, but they need adult supervision."[6]

The recognition of the need for supervision of the marketplace is at the heart of our current dilemma. In the past the proven solution was government supervision, but governments today cannot easily return to many of the forms of ownership, price regulation, and direct market controls that they have recently abandoned.

A Way Out

One way out of this apparently paradoxical situation is for government to create a marketplace that steers corporations toward a public good appropriate for today without direct government control—a kind of new version of the *invisible hand*. Adam Smith used this famous phrase only once in his classic economics text *The Wealth of Nations*, when he described a businessman pursuing profits as being "led by an invisible hand to promote an end which was no part of his intention." This man of business, as Smith described him, "neither intends to promote the public interest, nor knows how much he is promoting it," yet he is, in fact, doing so.[7]

Smith's metaphor of the invisible hand has led some to imagine a smoothly functioning economy independent of governmental guidance. Smith did protest the protectionist policies of the governments of his time and their granting of commercial monopolies, but he nevertheless saw a crucial role for government in establishing an orderly legal and societal infrastructure in which trade could function.[8] This hand was visible to those in government and its goal was clear: to achieve the public interest. Smith favored government's hand being used to encourage competition and limit monopolies.[9] He also believed it was important to limit business's influence on the legislative process. As he so eloquently put it, businessmen (whom he referred to as "those who live by profit") are "an order of men, whose interest is never exactly the same with that of the public, who have generally an interest to deceive and even oppress the public, and who accordingly have, upon many occasions, both deceived and oppressed it." He therefore advocated treating the involvement of businessmen in politics "not only with the most scrupulous, but with the most suspicious attention."[10]

What appears confusing and contradictory about the current situation is that the role of government needs to simultaneously expand and contract. Government is abandoning many direct controls of business in order to set corporations free to deliver goods and services more efficiently. At the same time, it needs to create new mechanisms to protect certain basic public interests. These public interests are captured in what I call *long-term wealth creation*. I will define what I mean by this term more clearly in the next chapter, but suffice it to say here that in many regards it is plain common sense. It is common sense that corporations should not be allowed to destroy the earth's protective ozone layer in the pursuit of profits. It is common sense that deregulated utilities should not be allowed to abandon their infrastructure, to cut off water or electricity to the poor, in the name of higher dividends. It is common sense that drug companies should not let populations be devastated by HIV/AIDS in order to protect a handful of profitable patents—and the public will not remain silent while they do so.

The Role of Socially Responsible Investing and Corporate Social Responsibility

In sum, the shifting of assets and power from government to business has led to a shift in the public's expectations of what both government and corporations should do. In particular, it raises questions about how governments can set the ground rules for a marketplace in which the players themselves act to direct corporations to serve the public interest. *The marketplace*, as I use the term here, encompasses the financial markets, the consumer markets, and the labor markets; *the players* I refer to are investors, consumers, employees, communities, and other corporate stakeholders.

I believe that the growing interest in SRI and CSR is attributable in large part to the desire to create this new invisible hand in the marketplace. These two fields are appealing because those working in them have gained valuable insights over the years operating at the intersections of market value and societal values, profits and wealth, self-interest and public concerns. They have wrestled with questions of what companies can do to create long-term wealth, what measurements might capture this value, how to assess the strength of corporations' relationships with stakeholders in addition to stockowners, how to address the complications of conflicting societal concerns, and what the market can do to reward those whose efforts are most successful in these broader realms.

Those working in the fields of SRI and CSR have pioneered concepts, research methodologies, and modes of interacting with corporations that can be helpful in the creation of a marketplace that effectively provides a guiding hand. Today we can glimpse the outlines of what such a marketplace might look like. But only a concerted effort by government—with the active support of investors, consumers, workers, the general public, and corporations themselves—can bring it into being. Societies around the world must understand the public interest that corporations can serve in order to create a solid infrastructure that compels the business community to work—deliberately or in spite of itself—toward that end. Bringing this about will require new data, new organizations to analyze that data, public debate about the data's significance, and the creation of consequences flowing from this analysis and debate. In the next chapter, we begin by examining what is the public interest that corporations can serve and taking a look at how some corporations today are serving it.

CHAPTER TWO

What Is Long-Term Wealth?

AS A FIRST STEP IN ADDRESSING THE CURRENT DILEMMA ABOUT corporations' relationship to society, this chapter defines and examines the public interest that corporations can best serve—what I call the creation of long-term wealth. Five companies that integrate this concept into their daily operations are described to illustrate its benefits. These profiles also highlight the ongoing challenges of long-term wealth creation, which can require astute management skills and undivided focus. This chapter also discusses why government, before it can create a transparent market that values and rewards such exceptional efforts, must first ensure, through legislation and regulation, that uncontrolled business does not abuse public wealth. At the same time, it must distinguish those services that it can best deliver as public goods from those that may be best delivered through the private markets.

Defining Long-Term Wealth

A definition of the public interest that corporations can best serve in today's world is the starting point for this discussion. I define that public interest here as: *the creation of value that will continue to benefit members of society even if the corporation were dissolved today.*

This definition builds on the familiar concept that corporations can create economic wealth that benefits society through productivity gains. As corporations innovate and increase efficiency, they generate wealth that raises overall prosperity to new levels. Having demonstrated their worth in the marketplace, corporations' technological and managerial innovations can transcend the life of the company to become part of society's wealth-generating capabilities.

Today, however, many investors, consumers, public policymakers, employees, and communities increasingly expect corporations to provide value that goes beyond simple efficiency increases. Their new definition of value qualifies the ways in which profits should be generated, and once generated, put to use. I call this value *long-term wealth*. Long-term wealth encompasses productivity gains and technological advances, but it also demands that the profits generated not be made at the expense of society or the environment and that they be productively reinvested for the benefit of the corporation's stakeholders.

As formulated here, this concept of long-term wealth is a variation on many of the ideas developed in a rich literature over the past three decades. Approaching the same idea from varying perspectives, advocates of the development of increasingly prosperous societies that can endure have promoted the concepts, among others, of sustainability (for example, John Elkington), natural capitalism (Paul Hawken), natural economics (Jane Jacobs), total wealth creation (Margaret Blair), social entrepreneurship (David Bornstein), blended value (Jed Emerson), civic stewardship (Marcy Murninghan), the open enterprise (Don Tapscott and David Ticoll), moral capitalism (Stephen Young), and the moral economy (William Greider).[1]

These and other authors have talked of the importance of developing human capital, community capital, and environmental capital (Jon Gunneman, for example) and have drawn analogies between the values of societal and financial wealth.[2] They also share many of the concerns of economists such as Amartya Sen, who stress society's obligation to provide citizens with crucial qualities of life in addition to raising income levels.[3]

My particular formulation of long-term wealth creation includes three expectations that proponents of SRI and CSR have come to consider as part of the corporation's obligations to society. They are that corporations:

- Do not externalize costs onto society.
- Do not deplete natural resources irretrievably.
- Do not impoverish stakeholders.

Or, to put it positively, corporations should do the following:

- Address and minimize the public costs they incur before they declare private profits.
- Preserve and renew resources so that they remain available for future generations.
- Invest in stakeholder relations, including, but not limited to, their stockowners.

In concrete terms, corporations that pursue long-term wealth creation might, for example, do these things: invest in employee training that prepares workers not only for their current jobs but for future employment as well; develop a community's capacity to provide child care not only for their own employees but for other community members; pay their fair share of taxes so that local governments can provide infrastructure and education in their communities, even if that means reduced profits for stockowners; educate employees on retirement planning, even if they are not required to do so by law; preserve biodiversity and implement energy efficiency programs, even if the payback may be difficult to justify in the short run; require vendors and suppliers to implement credible quality or environmental management systems, even if that means increased prices; and ensure access to capital for underserved communities or entrepreneurs, even if they may ultimately become new competitors. Although not necessarily in corporations' narrowly defined, short-term interests, these initiatives create lasting societal value.

Conversely, corporations that destroy long-term wealth might do the following: compensate management excessively, asserting that the marketplace demands such salaries and bonuses; fail to provide adequate pensions for their employees, pointing out that their peers do no better; extract tax breaks that exceed the quantifiable benefits that their presence provides local communities simply because they have the power to do so; refuse to implement a comprehensive environmental management system on the grounds that they have no such legal obligation; encourage consumption of "supersized" portions of unhealthy food or promote the sale of unnecessarily expensive, patent-protected drugs because these marketing opportunities are irresistible; provide products or services that are potentially addictive, such as tobacco and gambling, without confronting their harmful effects; or ignore the potentially adverse long-term effects of burning fossil fuels in the face of overwhelming evidence of global harm. Although not illegal, such corporate actions leave society the poorer.

The definition of long-term wealth as conceived here can be expressed as a formula: start with the value of a company's contributions to society through productivity gains and innovation (less any costs it imposes through anticompetitive practices), add to it the value of the company's internalization of social costs (less its externalized costs), plus the value of its sustainable management of environmental resources (less the costs of its environmental harms), plus the value created through its investments in stakeholder relations (less any costs created by mismanagement or neglect of these relations).

Expressing this concept through such a formula raises a number of important questions, however. What does it mean for a company to internalize costs, manage for sustainability, or invest in the value of its stakeholders? How easily can companies achieve these goals? To what extent can these efforts be meaningfully quantified? What is the proper role of government in supporting these efforts? What is the role of the marketplace in their cultivation? Why are these issues of crucial importance today?

Five Examples of Long-Term Wealth Creation

To answer the first of these questions, let's begin by looking at five corporations, each of which exemplifies one element of the preceding equation: Organic Valley (internalization of costs), Patagonia (commitment to environmental sustainability), and Springfield Remanufacturing, Wainwright Bank, and Timberland (investments in stakeholders – employees, customers, and communities, respectively).[4]

Organic Valley Family of Farms

Organic Valley Family of Farms is a cooperative of dairy and other farmers headquartered in rural LaFarge, Wisconsin, with over six hundred participating members in eighteen states around the country. The co-op was founded in 1988 by George Siemon who, after fifteen years as a farmer devoted to organic principles, joined with a half-dozen of his peers to create the Coulee Region Organic Produce Pool. From this modest beginning grew Organic Valley Family of Farms, which in 2003 had $156 million in revenues (and projected 2004 revenues of over $200 million) and whose farmers managed ninety-five thousand acres of land organically.

Organic Valley has taken the exceptional step of internalizing some of the costs that large-scale, chemical-dependent agribusiness often imposes on society. The food products that today's agribusiness brings to the supermarket shelves at low cost to consumers can come at a high cost to society in the form of an increasingly contaminated water supply, deteriorating soil quality, and wetlands damaged by overuse of fertilizers and pesticides. Moreover, these giant firms' economies of scale make small-scale, local land ownership increasingly difficult. To avoid this externalization of costs onto society, Organic Valley pro-motes the adoption of small-scale organic farming techniques.

A major challenge for its small farmers, however, is that in a volatile commodity market, where conventional milk is often priced more cheaply than its organic counterpart, those who adopt organic farming practices run the risk of being priced out of business. Organic Valley has developed a two-pronged solution to this problem. First, the co-op's elected board of directors meets annually to set a fair and stable price for their products—that is, a predictable, minimum price that the co-op will pay for the year, independent from the swings of the com-modity market. With the assurance of this stable price, the co-op's farm-ers can continue their organic practices and manage their farms at a reasonable profit. In recent years that price at times has been as much as 40 percent above that of the commodity market.

An additional benefit to co-op members is their ability to market their products collectively under the Organic Valley brand name, which offers a guarantee to the consumer on product quality, environmental values, and local land ownership. Through an extensive distribution network, the co-op's products are available throughout the United States, as well as in Canada and Japan. These policies and practices help insulate small-scale organic farmers from the pressures of the commod-ity markets created by large-scale agribusiness that would otherwise not allow them to serve consumers committed to sustainable agriculture. Meanwhile, their organic farms create a long-term societal wealth in the form of enriched soil, clean water, and a network of independent agri-cultural entrepreneurs.

Patagonia, Inc.

Founded in the early 1970s and headquartered in Ventura, Cali-fornia, Patagonia, Inc., is a high-profile outdoor apparel company with approximately $230 million in revenues in 2003. The company is a rare example of a firm that has been willing to gamble its financial future on a company-wide commitment to environmental sustainability. It made this gamble most dramatically in 1996 when its founder, Yvon Chouinard, recognized that his commitment to the environment was being undercut by the company's use of conventionally grown cotton, one of the most chemically dependent of crops. At that time, the company decided to convert the cotton in its entire product line to organic. Its commitment to do so, however, forced it to cut its sportswear line by one-third because of limitations on the amount of high-quality organic cotton then available, at a cost of approximately $20 million in lost sales.

Patagonia has since gone on to become a highly successful promoter of organic cotton throughout the sports apparel industry, even among its competitors such as Nike and Mountain Equipment Co-op. In addition, its Beneficial T's program produces T-shirt "blanks," as well as tote bags and hats, with 100 percent organic cotton content. The company makes these items available to clothing designers throughout the apparel industry. As of 2004 the Beneficial T's program was using about five hundred thousand pounds of organic cotton annually.

The switch to organic cotton was one of the boldest steps in the firm's company-wide efforts to implement environmental programs, but not the only one. In 1993 Patagonia worked with one of its suppliers to develop technology that could produce fleece fabric from recycled plastic soda bottles. In a similar initiative in 2004, it introduced a filament partially made from recycled plastic into the yarns used in clothing such as running shorts and rain shells. Similarly in the energy area, in constructing its distribution center in Reno, Nevada, it incorporated energy-efficient lighting systems that provide 30 percent savings on energy bills and radiant heating systems that generate savings of approximately 15 percent. Its Reno outlet store uses solar panels to generate electricity. Its thirteen buildings in California purchase electricity from renewable energy plants.

Through two exceptional policies, Patagonia also supports the environmental movement more generally. Today, employees who have been with the firm for two years can take an eight-week paid leave (with benefits) to work with environmental organizations. In addition, the company donates 1 percent of its sales to environmental causes, a generous and highly unusual approach to charitable giving. (Most companies pledge a percentage of profits, rather than sales, to charity.) Through this program, Patagonia has made $20 million in gifts to environmental organizations to date. To promote similar environmental giving programs, Yvon Chouinard was instrumental in the founding of 1 Percent for the Planet, an alliance of thirty-three businesses, mostly small firms that have made similar pledges, which through December 2003 had donated $1.7 million to environmental causes.

Springfield Remanufacturing Corporation

A manufacturing firm headquartered in Springfield, Missouri, Springfield Remanufacturing Corporation (SRC) has survived and thrived in large part because of its willingness to invest in its employees. In the mid-1980s, this remanufacturer of automotive components was a division of International Harvester, then on the brink of bankruptcy. Rather than see his division close down, its manager, Jack Stack, persuaded corporate headquarters to sell the business to its employees. Stack then began the painstaking process of educating the new owners about the business of running a business. They were taught financials, budgeting, cost management, and operations. They learned to grapple with difficult decisions about allocation of resources to debt repayment, investments in technology, and payouts to owners.

Today, with a total of some eight hundred employee-owners at twelve principal subsidiaries and revenues of approximately $200 million in 2003, SRC is a profitable holding company operating multiple related firms. Upon joining the firm, each new employee participates in a two-day workshop on open book management and subsequently takes part in weekly "huddles"; in these staff meetings, the financials of the subsidiary's operations, as well as the financials of other subsidiaries, are shared and discussed. In addition, the management teams of all the subsidiaries meet every two weeks to share financial information that they then communicate back to their teams. SRC also holds quarterly financial literacy workshops, which were attended by approximately 120 company members annually as of 2004. Most recently, SRC has invested in educating its employees on the issue of health care costs. As part of this program, it has hired a part-time fitness instructor and a part-time wellness coordinator. These efforts resulted in a 33 percent reduction in health care costs for the firm in the first six months of 2004.

SRC believes that investments in open book management, with its ability to empower employees, can have long-term benefits for other firms as well. Consequently, it has established a subsidiary called the Great Game of Business, named after Stack's book on the subject.[5] This consulting and training firm provides a range of assessment, training, and coaching services on open book management to approximately three hundred companies each year. Its annual National Gathering of Games, a three-day conference dedicated to open book management, had approximately 350 attendees in 2004.

Wainwright Bank & Trust Company

Wainwright Bank & Trust Company is a Boston-based bank with approximately $625 million in assets as of 2003. It has chosen to focus its business particularly on strengthening those in need in its local community, where it is the bank of choice for many social service organizations. From the early 1990s through 2004, it lent $11 million to organizations providing housing for persons with AIDS and $15 million to those serving the homeless, as well as $75 million to affordable housing agencies. During that time, it made some $350 million in community development loans. Wainwright maintains a four-person team in its lending department; this team specializes in loans to community service organizations.

Wainwright has also invested in its customer base in ways that go beyond simply providing a needed service at a reasonable price. The bank includes on its own Web site a section called CommunityRoom .net. There, local nonprofit clients can maintain individual Web pages (over one hundred as of 2004) describing their activities. The Web site is set up so that through it individuals can make donations directly to these organizations, and in 2003 the site generated approximately $250,000 in donations for these groups. (Donations were running at double that rate as of mid-2004.) The bank's brick-and-mortar branches also have rooms set aside for use by community groups that are accessible at all times. The bank's most recent branch features a "cybercafe" in the lobby, with a fireplace, a plasma-screen TV, free coffee and doughnuts, and Internet access available at no cost to members of the community, whether or not they are bank customers.

Wainwright has also made an exceptional commitment to the local gay and lesbian community. It was one of the original sponsors of Boston's Gay Pride parade in 1993 and the lead sponsor in 2004. It was among the first publicly traded companies in the United States to have an openly lesbian member on its board of directors. Its top management has frequently spoken out on gay and lesbian rights, and for many years the bank offered an affinity credit card (such cards donate a percentage of revenues to charitable causes) that gave a portion of the amounts charged to organizations serving gay and lesbian communities and organizations working with the homeless.

The Timberland Company

Many companies have employee volunteer programs, but few have worked to make a spirit of service to the community a part of the corporate culture as thoroughly as the Timberland Company. Founded in 1918 and headquartered in Stratham, New Hampshire, this manufacturer of footwear and apparel had approximately $1.3 billion in 2003 revenues. Through a program called Path of Service, employees can spend up to 40 hours each year volunteering with social service organizations on company time. Since the inception of this program, employees have logged over 250,000 hours in volunteer time.

The company has focused its volunteering particularly on City Year, a Boston-based urban Peace Corps–style organization for the young (between seventeen and twenty-four years of age) that served as a model for President Clinton's Americorps national service program. Founded in Boston in 1988, City Year now has programs in fourteen communities around the country. Its diverse pool of 750 participants take part each year in programs of community service, leadership development, and civic engagement. In 2001, City Year launched its Clinton Democracy Fellowship program, which brings to the United States young leaders from other countries who are committed to citizen service and social entrepreneurship.

Since 1992, Timberland has been a major supporter of City Year, identifying itself publicly with the organization. During that time, it has donated some $20 million in goods and services to City Year, including employee volunteer time and clothing in the form of a City Year uniform. Timberland's CEO, Jeffrey Swartz, serves on the organization's board of directors, and the City Year New Hampshire Corps is housed at the company's headquarters. In addition, Timberland regularly contracts with City Year staff for training in volunteerism and diversity awareness. Timberland's commitment to civic involvement also sets the tone for the company's strong initiatives on environmental and overseas labor issues throughout its operations.

I have chosen these five smaller companies here to illustrate how a firm's identity can be bound up in exceptional commitments to creating long-term wealth. But many larger companies are also committed to creating long-term wealth that transcends technological innovation or increases in efficiency. For example, since the early 1990s, through its funding for dependent care, International Business Machines Corporation (IBM) has invested in the child care and elder care infrastructures of communities where its plants are located. IBM was also instrumental in the formation of the American Business Collaborative for Quality Dependent Care in 1992, through which it and a coalition of other companies—including Abbott Laboratories, ExxonMobil, General Electric, Johnson & Johnson, and Texas Instruments—have invested over $135 million in these infrastructures around the country. The purpose of this program is not only to create long-lasting solutions to the dependent care needs for company employees but also to help solve this problem for their surrounding communities.

In another example of the kind of long-term wealth that large firms can create, Starbucks Corporation, in partnership with Conservation International, developed a set of coffee-sourcing guidelines in 2001 that define a category of preferred suppliers to which Starbucks turns first for its purchases and from which it is willing to accept higher prices. To qualify, these preferred suppliers must meet certain quality, social, and environmental criteria. The greater their verifiable commitments to set goals in these areas, the higher their status as preferred vendors. This program supports coffee farmers who are part of a sustainable society.

Organizations such as San Francisco–based Business for Social Responsibility, which is dedicated to promoting responsible business practices, and recent books such as *Profits with Principles* by Ira Jackson and Jane Nelson have documented and continue to encourage similar efforts by many larger corporations.[6]

Encouraging and Assessing Wealth Creation

These examples illustrate both the appeal of wealth creation and its challenges. As we have seen, companies that look to the long term can create value that would persist even if they went out of business tomorrow: Organic Valley would leave a legacy of enriched farmland, Patagonia would leave a strengthened organic cotton industry, Springfield Remanufacturing would leave workers who are trained to understand and manage a business, Wainwright Bank would leave a strengthened customer base of social service organizations, and Timberland would leave a broadly shared sense of service and community. These are valuable assets that have strong appeal.

These examples are also helpful in making several broader points that illustrate the challenges of long-term wealth creation. These are initiatives at companies that today enjoy reasonable profitability. But integrating long-term wealth creation into business operations is not an automatic guarantee of rewards in the marketplace. It is a complicated task that requires good business sense, strong management skills, and financial resources. One of the favorites of the SRI community in the mid-1980s was Digital Equipment Corporation, whose employee and community relations were in many senses exemplary. Through various business missteps it fell on hard financial times and was eventually acquired by Compaq Computer (in turn acquired by Hewlett-Packard Company). More recently, AstroPower, one of the few publicly traded corporations focused on the commercialization of solar power technologies, appealed to many social investors. However, it suffered financially and in October 2004 declared bankruptcy and agreed to be acquired by General Electric. Astute business judgments and effective management skills are necessary to make these often complicated and groundbreaking efforts pay off in the marketplace.

These examples also illustrate the point that the generation of long-term wealth, when executed throughout a firm, requires single-minded focus. Internalizing even a single societal cost, such as Organic Valley has done, can be a challenging business proposition that pays off only if the market is persuaded that the resulting product carries additional value. Attempting to sustain a single natural resource, as Patagonia has done, can require a company to gamble its financial future as it ventures into untried territory. Empowering workers to understand the basics of business and financial decision making, as Springfield Remanufacturing has done, is a costly, ongoing effort that will bring rewards only if employees are motivated to apply their newfound skills productively. The demands of even a single effort may mean—as the authors of the book *Built to Last* and other works on the characteristics of enduring and successful corporate cultures point out—that these companies "tend to have only a few core values" on which they build their business and which remain central to their identity over time.[7]

One of the implications of this need to focus is that companies engaged in long-term wealth creation should not necessarily be expected to excel in everything they do. There is a tendency among those approaching the concept of socially responsible business to want to find only angels—or devils—when it comes to CSR records. The fact that a company with an exceptional commitment in one area chooses not to make extraordinary efforts in all others is not a cause for alarm.

Companies' stories are multifaceted, and finding excellence in one or two areas is difficult enough in and of itself. Moreover, companies change, new issues emerge, and difficult situations arise. Thinking of companies as either all good or all bad is often an approach that fails to comprehend the complexities of business and its relationship to society, a fact that is as true for small companies with limited resources as for large companies with their multiple management challenges.

These general observations will inform our discussion further in part 2 when we examine the difficulties of the current financial and consumer marketplaces in quantifying and judging the value of these considerable efforts in wealth creation and in rewarding them consistently. However, before we turn to the question of how today's marketplace can be transformed to achieve these goals, we need to address briefly government's role outside the marketplace in ensuring that the fundamentals of societal wealth are not destroyed or abused by unscrupulous corporations. These steps are necessary to create the level playing field that corporations need to compete fairly and transparently in these areas.

Relative Roles of Government and the Marketplace

The first step that government must take, before it attempts to create a marketplace that directs the private sector toward the public interest, is to enact and enforce laws and regulations that prevent the most blatant destruction of long-term wealth. Today's governments make many corporate activities illegal because they impose unacceptable costs. Engaging in price fixing, marketing unsafe products, operating unsafe work environments, manufacturing ozone-depleting chemicals, publishing inaccurate financial statements, and discriminating in the workplace are all illegal because they impose unacceptably high costs on society. Their costs are unacceptably high no matter how beneficial they might be to individual company profits. Government cannot wait for the marketplace to prevent or correct such abuse, nor can it rely on the marketplace to do so.

A second duty of government is to distinguish between public and private goods. A detailed discussion of this important subject is beyond the scope of this book—but I will observe that long-term wealth creation, as I use the term, is provided by the private sector, whereas the term *public goods* refers to what the public sector delivers. Corporations' ability to generate long-term wealth should not be confused with governments' obligations to provide public goods.[8]

This distinction can be confusing, because the further out one looks, the more long-term wealth can resemble public goods. The two, however, are not the same. There are activities for which government will judge the for-profit sector ill-suited. For example, few would argue that corporations should provide basic public goods such as the legal system, public safety, national defense, or roads, sewers, and other infrastructure. Yet as the pendulum has swung in recent years from government toward the private sector, corporations have begun increasingly to experiment with supplying services that were traditionally in the public domain, such as prison management, primary education, and military support services.[9] Moreover, it is often a matter of ongoing debate as to what role government should play in such areas as providing health care, supporting postsecondary education, maintaining cultural institutions, assuring the availability of public utilities, and so on.

Debates about these issues are a sign of a healthy and open society. These debates may be played out through experimentation in the marketplace, but ultimately it is government's role to determine which goods and services should be public and which should be private. Where one national government or another draws the line will vary, but once that line has been drawn, the concept of long-term wealth generation can be usefully applied to activities that are allocated to the private sector and should not be confused with government-provided public goods. Indeed, the debate about whether particular corporate activities can create long-term wealth can be a help as government grapples with issues of which activities belong in the public sphere and which in the private.

Once government has established a level playing field and distinguishes the public from the private, the marketplace then can be particularly useful—but currently isn't constructed to be particularly effective—in encouraging positive and innovative initiatives that create long-term wealth. Encouraging corporations to pay increased attention to energy efficiency and conservation, to balance work and family considerations for their employees, to shift to organic agriculture, to support local communities and help them create strong infrastructures, to monitor the labor practices of their foreign vendors—all are examples of areas of clear benefit to society, but for which direct regulations can be problematic and for which rewards through the marketplace can consequently be particularly useful.

In addition, the marketplace can play a catalytic role where corporate activities are not illegal but there is debate about their benefit or harm, or when government has chosen not to act to correct such harm. Tobacco products are legal, but even when used as intended and in moderation can impose health care costs on society. When pharmaceutical companies lobby to extend patent protections on their drugs or to prevent the marketing of cheaper versions of HIV/AIDS medications, they are acting legally but make health care unnecessarily expensive or deprive those without resources of much-needed care. Aggressive marketing of sports utility vehicles is legal but can increase fatal crashes because of their design and contribute to health and environmental problems for the general public because of their fuel inefficiency. Paying a minimum wage that is not a living wage is legal but can create a class of the working poor, for whom society must bear the cost of social services.

Similarly, there are often profound debates in a society about whether new technologies and business practices are creating or destroying long-term wealth. For example, as agribusinesses aggressively pursue genetically modified plants and foods, corporations generally see little potential for harm while many governments, scientists, and individuals around the world are not sure whether genetically altered hormones, food crops, and cotton will feed and clothe the poor or threaten the viability of agriculture for future generations. Similarly, the success of Wal-Mart and other "big box" stores raises a divisive issue as to whether the unrelenting drive to provide goods at the lowest possible price is providing poor communities with exactly what they need at prices they can afford or destroying communities and impoverishing workers.

In these cases, a fully informed, properly constructed marketplace has the potential to play a valuable role by airing issues publicly, assessing the potential for future costs or liabilities, and generally pushing corporations to reform or pushing government to further action. It will take a special effort by government along with investors, consumers, and corporations themselves to transform today's marketplaces into new vehicles that can reasonably and successfully analyze issues of long-term wealth and encourage its creation. Transfers of assets and power from government to corporations can capitalize on business's efficiency and innovation, but only if the marketplaces are set up to influence them where government chooses not to, or is ill-suited to apply systematic pressure.

By 2050, in a world of nine billion technologically advanced people, the margins for error will be considerably slimmer than they are today. Only if government and the marketplaces coordinate to work in an effective and balanced manner toward an enduring society will social and environment crises of substantial proportions be avoided. When and how best to use the marketplace so that corporations can be directed to these ends as part of that effort is a question that the SRI and CSR movements have explored from various angles in recent years. Chapter 3 looks at the strengths and limitations of three of the current approaches.

CHAPTER THREE

Guiding the Corporation

OVER THE PAST THREE DECADES, THOSE WORKING IN THE socially responsible investing and corporate social responsibility fields have developed three principal strategies to persuade businesses to act in the public interest. These strategies overlap to a certain extent but each can be examined separately to illustrate the strengths and limitations of its approach: (1) *the business case* helps companies see how increasing efficiency and profits can coincide with creating social benefits; (2) *values-driven models* seek to persuade corporate managers to act ethically in accordance with accepted social norms, rather than simply increase profits by any legal means; and (3) *systems of measurement and rewards* evaluate the performance of businesses in creating societal value—that is, long-term wealth, as described in the previous chapter—and reward those that succeed in doing so.

Ultimately, all three strategies can be used to help persuade corporate managers to move toward the shared goal of broad-based wealth creation. I believe that the third strategy is particularly useful because it allows a wide spectrum of investors, consumers, and other stakeholders to send informed, consistent messages on social and environmental issues to managers through the financial mechanisms of the marketplace. This chapter will take a look at all three.

The Business Case

Underlying the business case for companies to act in socially responsible ways is the assertion that they can generate profits by increasing their efficiency and productivity while simultaneously taking actions that serve broader social interests. Companies taking this approach will profit while society benefits, and for that reason those who make this case often describe it as "doing well while doing good."

The business case works best when short-term paybacks and profits are clearly quantifiable. For example, investments in energy efficiency can drop rapidly to the bottom line. Reduced use of toxic chemicals in manufacturing can immediately lower disposal costs. Employee training can quickly increase productivity. Better product quality can increase customer loyalty and undercut competition. Involving employees in problem solving and tying pay to profits can increase efficiency and reduce employee turnover, as can human resource programs that balance the demands of the workplace and family. Such initiatives eliminate current inefficiencies and result in quantifiable gains.

One strength of the business case is that it speaks the language of today's corporations; it fits naturally into current management strategies. Progressive corporations promoting CSR often advocate the business case. For example, Switzerland-based World Business Council for Sustainable Development (WBCSD), which promotes the pursuit of sustainable development among its 170 members, urges increased attention to such issues as ecoefficiency, corporate social responsibility, biodiversity, and innovation, pointing out that each of them can help the bottom line.[1]

The business case also works in the marketplace as it is currently conceived. If socially beneficial initiatives can generate cost savings, then corporations undertaking them can continue to compete for consumers on price and for investors on the prospects of increasing profitability. Similarly, there is little need for further government intervention, because the profit motive will presumably drive companies to implement these kinds of initiatives on their own; the marketplace as it is structured today provides adequate rewards for doing so. To make this model work, corporate managers merely need to be persuaded to work smarter and to embrace a "double" or "triple" bottom line that encompasses social and environmental as well as financial goals.

Although the business case works effectively to persuade corporate managers to undertake positive initiatives in many situations, it has two limitations. First, its ability to persuade is unclear in situations where companies can make short-term profits while harming the public interest— that is, externalizing costs, exploiting resources, or abusing stakeholders. It also provides little guidance when doing what is in society's interest has a payback period that is so long term and diffuse that there is no business case for doing it in any usual sense of the term. The business case can thus leave unresolved tensions between pure profit and broader societal benefit. It helps corporate managers know what to do when short-term profits and the public interest coincide, but it does not provide guidance when they don't.

The corporate world today abounds with examples of companies profiting in the short run by externalizing costs, jeopardizing natural resources, and acting counter to stakeholders' interests. It is difficult, for example, to see how marketing tobacco products could be seen as doing well while doing good. It is difficult to convince many in the fishing industry that restricting their catch, although good for the ocean's fishing stocks and the environment, will benefit them as well in the short run. Disputes between environmentalists and the business world over restrictions in the name of protecting endangered species are similarly hard to resolve. And food companies that promote oversized servings of unhealthy food or automobile manufacturers that aggressively market SUVs encourage overconsumption of products with public costs while they rack up short-term profits.

The business case is also of limited use when a company must look far into the future for its rewards, or when investments with long-term societal benefits cut into short-term profits. On the simplest level, this is a question of payback periods. If a manager is presented with several opportunities to make energy-saving investments, she will naturally choose the ones that bring the greatest savings the most quickly. But where should she draw the line as the prospects for cost savings recede into the future? A well-trained and healthy workforce will give a company a competitive advantage, but as advantageous as this is for both the company and society, there is a limit to what a company will spend. It is not always clear when a decision to limit these expenditures makes reasonable and ethical business sense.

This question of long-term rewards versus short-term profits shows up in other forms as well. For example, what is the business case for paying taxes or for encouraging competition? It is possible to make the business case for both these basic requirements of a smoothly functioning economy. In the former case, business cannot function effectively unless government is funded to provide the legal and financial infrastructure that allows business to generate profits. As for the latter, corporations in general may be more profitable if competition drives them to create a wealthy society through productivity gains. However, these considerations are so broad and long term that they are of only general use to corporate managers. They tell managers that their company should pay some taxes and welcome some competition, but they give little guidance on how much of either is appropriate. Put differently, to make the business case in these situations, consideration of what looks like long-term wealth becomes the driving force, rather than the short-term profits on which the business case is often based. Thus, the business case works well in situations where there is a convergence of long-term public and short-term private interests, but it encounters difficulties when the two conflict.

Values-Driven Models

Values-driven models are a valuable tool that will be part of any solution to the problem of how to direct corporations to the public interest. Business managers who embrace values-driven models bring commonly accepted moral and ethical considerations to the table when making their daily decisions. Based on shared visions, codes, and standards, these models help drive change in corporate cultures and align business decisions with societal norms. An increasing number of companies have adopted this approach.[2]

A rich array of tools has evolved over the past three decades to help companies integrate values-driven models into their management practices, including corporate vision statements, mission statements, and statements of values that set aspirational goals and help mold the corporate culture. Internal business codes of conduct and accompanying corporate ethics programs are also increasingly important management tools. They often address complex situations involving conflicts of interest, bribery, or questionable marketing practices.

In addition to these individual corporate efforts, an increasing number of nongovernmental organizations and quasi-governmental bodies have developed codes and standards for best practices that cut across industries. Similarly, industry-specific guidelines now set standards for behavior in particularly controversial areas, such as labor practices in the apparel industry, environmental policies in bank lending, and sustainable forestry and agriculture practices. Finally, a growing number of standards-setting and certification bodies provide companies with detailed methodologies for the implementation of quality controls, labor practices, and environmental protection.

Internal guidelines developed by corporations themselves, such as mission statements and codes of conduct, are important in driving change in corporations and setting internal cultural norms. When CEOs include broad societal values among their top priorities, these guidelines can set the tone for an entire organization and align its public mission with specific business practices. At Vermont-based Green Mountain Coffee Roasters, for example, CEO Bob Stiller states: "A key component of Green Mountain Coffee's business philosophy is doing the right thing locally, globally, and for the environment."[3] At Timber-land, headquartered in New Hampshire, CEO Jeffrey Swartz asserts: "I'm interested in how a business can be a vehicle for social justice."[4] And Johnson & Johnson's well-known "Credo" preserves its founder's values as a part of the corporate culture.

Externally developed codes and standards are valuable as well. They provide guidance in morally ambiguous situations or when corporate managers may be unclear on acceptable norms. In recent years, such principles have proven their worth. In the 1980s, for example, the Reverend Leon Sullivan's Statement of Principles for South Africa helped corporations operating in that country both improve their labor standards there and work toward ending its apartheid system. More recently, environmental certification and ecolabeling programs have set standards for companies wishing to move to more sustainable business practices.

The increasing willingness of corporations to use the language of values-driven models in communicating with their stakeholders and the general public is a reflection of the public's new expectation that corporations act in society's interest. But despite their considerable virtues, values-driven approaches raise several difficult questions. First, how do investors, consumers, and the general public know when corporations are actually living up to their stated goals? Second, in a world of proliferating codes of conduct and calls for corporations to act morally, how do managers prioritize among equally legitimate claims? Finally, what is the relationship between these visions, codes, and standards and the proper functioning of a watchful government?

How Can Corporate Conduct Be Verified?

As an increasing number of companies publicly state their commitment to values, codes, and standards, there is a corresponding increase in demand for outside assurance that these commitments are real. Some view these commitments as no more than exercises in green-washing or attempts to buy public goodwill at no real cost. Skeptics are likely to continue to question such corporate claims until credible verification processes are developed.

But commitments to general, broadly defined values are difficult to verify. For example, Johnson & Johnson's Credo is widely recognized and praised for its strong commitment to public values. It speaks of "fair and adequate" compensation for employees, "fair profit" for suppliers, a "fair share of taxes" to government, and a "fair return" to stockowners.[5] The Credo has served Johnson & Johnson well over the years and helped make the company one of the most admired in the United States today. The commitments embodied in its Credo demonstrate a sensitivity to issues of justice and a sense of balance that are remarkable in today's corporate world. It is nevertheless difficult to know exactly what such general commitments mean to a company or to verify when a company is living up to its standards.

Indeed, for less well-intentioned companies, values statements can be meaningless gestures, mere exercises in hypocrisy. For example, in its 2000 annual report Enron made this statement: "We are satisfied with nothing less than the very best in everything we do. We will continue to raise the bar for everyone. The great fun here will be for all of us to discover just how good we can really be."[6]

Standards-setting and certification processes offer a valuable form of verification when more industry-specific or issue-specific codes are involved. A wide range of such schemes have grown up over the past three decades, promoted variously by government, industry, and environmental and civil society organizations. Generally speaking, they take a multistakeholder approach to developing these standards and verifying those companies that meet them. The International Organization for Standardization (ISO), based in Switzerland, is one of the better known of these organizations. Its ISO 14000 standards, for example, certify that companies' plants have implemented rigorous environmental management processes. The ISO 9000 certification series for quality processes has been widely adopted throughout industry. In June 2004, ISO announced that it would develop guidelines for corporate CSR programs, but would not seek to certify such programs.[7]

In one innovative recent approach, the International Social and Environmental Accreditation and Labeling (ISEAL) Alliance has formed a coalition of standards-setting, certification, and accreditation organizations that focus on social and environmental issues. Its members include the Fairtrade Labeling Organizations International, Forest Stewardship Council, International Federation of Organic Agriculture Movements, Marine Stewardship Council, Rainforest Alliance, and Social Accountability International, among others. In 2004, ISEAL published its Code of Good Practice for Setting Social and Environmental Standards, which sets standards for standard setting. ISEAL has also initiated the Social Accountability in Sustainable Agriculture project, which coordinates various organizations' work on certification and standards-setting for sustainable agriculture. Other important certification programs have also been established through various governmental, nongovernmental, and industry bodies.[8]

Certification and standards-setting programs are extremely helpful in establishing which corporations have met basic standards and in raising the bar for corporate conduct. They help investors and consumers who are concerned about specific social and environmental issues in their decision making. They have some limitations, however. They act as a kind of on/off switch—indicating when a company either qualifies or doesn't qualify against a fixed set of measurements, but usually not distinguishing further among firms that so qualify. This can limit debate in the sense that qualified companies all look the same through this lens. In addition, standards-setting and certification systems often provide few details on actual performance. Without detailed information on actual performance, it is difficult for investors, consumers, and others to know which among the qualified companies deserve greater or lesser rewards.

Which Values Should Businesses Adopt?

A second challenge in using values to drive corporations to act in the public interest is ambiguity about which values to espouse. One solution is for businesses to adopt internationally accepted codes or agreements that embody widely accepted norms. The International Labor Organization (ILO), for example, has developed a comprehensive set of standards for labor practices since its founding in 1919. Through a tripartite process of negotiations between labor, business, and national governments, ILO standards have become widely accepted.

The appeal of these multistakeholder codes and standards is strong, and corporations in increasing numbers are turning to them for guidance. The success of these codes, however, has created a related challenge: How are managers to choose among the proliferating numbers of such codes? For example, several codes for general corporate conduct have gained widespread recognition in recent years. The Organization for Economic Cooperation and Development (OECD) Guidelines for Multinational Enterprises, the United Nations Global Compact, the Global Sullivan Principles of Social Responsibility, and the Caux Round Table Principles for Business are all widely respected, but differ in certain key regards. At an industry level, codes are proliferating too. Between 2000 and 2003, three sets of environmental standards for financial services corporations were promulgated: the London Principles of Sustainable Finance developed for the Corporation of London by the Forum for the Future's Centre for Sustainable Investment, the Collevecchio Declaration on Financial Institutions and Sustainability endorsed by a worldwide coalition of over one hundred environmental activist and nonprofit organizations, and the Equator

Principles developed by a coalition of banks working in conjunction with the World Bank's International Finance Corporation. Also during that time the Global Reporting Initiative published its Financial Sector Reporting Guidelines, which, although not presented as a formal code of conduct, guide financial services companies to issues of general social and environmental concern. These efforts have been undertaken in addition to the U.N. Environmental Program's Financial Initiative, which has been working on similar issues since the mid-1990s with the backing of many of the world's largest financial services companies.

Corporate managers are thus confronted with a great variety of initiatives from which to choose, each with its own emphasis and each demanding its own commitments. The array of codes now being promulgated can be bewildering, both to companies and to the investors and consumers seeking to evaluate them. To cope with this problem, guides to these codes are being published and consultants are working with corporate managers to help them navigate the increasingly crowded field.[9]

Managers must also choose among the competing claims of corporate stakeholders. Value systems and codes of conduct are useful in helping management identify stakeholders—employees, consumers, communities, the environment—and their concerns but they do not help managers prioritize among these stakeholders. A forward-looking U.S. company may wish to offer employees profit sharing, make contributions to its local communities, and increase stockholders' dividends. These stakeholders are competing for a share of a single source of money. Codes and values don't provide metrics or principles for judgment on how to allocate among them. Managers' personal values, sense of fairness, or measurements of broadly conceived returns thus have to come into play in such exercises.

What Is the Relationship Between Codes of Conduct and Government?

Finally, values-driven models have an ambiguous relationship with the regulatory powers of national governments. The ambiguity stems in part from their success. They offer government an attractive alternative to heavy-handed regulation and they offer civil society an attractive alternative when national government lacks even basic oversight capabilities. But it is fair to ask whether these alternatives may at some point delay or discourage appropriate government action.

Multinational apparel companies, for example, are increasingly working with suppliers around the world to raise labor standards. Labor rights and human rights advocates have urged them to do so, particularly in countries where local managers do not have the skills to improve conditions or the national government lacks the regulatory infrastructure or resources it needs to effectively monitor and ameliorate working conditions. The resulting improvements in working conditions are desirable and praiseworthy. However, an overreliance on foreign-based corporations to monitor local practices through codes of conduct could create unintended consequences—for example, the local government may be tempted to delay, or cede to others, the development of an effective regulatory system to avoid shouldering this often expensive burden.

In sum, values-driven models are effective in driving internal change in the corporate world and raising the bar for standard industry practices. But they need to be supplemented with systems that verify performance, have flexible and graded reward mechanisms, help business managers choose among apparently equally legitimate claims on their resources, and encourage a role for national government in controlling abuses.

Systems of Measurement and Rewards

Systems of measurement and rewards based on the concept of long-term wealth creation provide a valuable complement and supplement to both the business case and values-driven models. The goal is to measure and judge the relative success of corporations in creating forms of long-term wealth and then use market mechanisms to reward them appropriately. This approach presupposes ongoing public debates and a process of valuation in the marketplace of the different forms of wealth creation. It also presupposes a means to communicate these debates and valuations to corporations effectively.

In their book *Redefining the Corporation*, James Post, Lee Preston, and Sybille Sachs describe a system in which assessments of the strength of corporations' stakeholder relations are the basis for their valuation in the marketplace. They argue that a corporation's ability to generate long-term wealth is tied directly to the strength of its stakeholder relations:

> All the firm's resources are represented in some way by various stakeholders, and it is the firm's relationships with stakeholders that make resources available to the organization. . . . It is the dynamic interaction with customers, employees, suppliers, investors, and other stakeholders that generates the organizational capacity to generate wealth over time. That is the central implication of the stakeholder view for strategic management. The failure to establish and maintain productive relationships with all of the firm's stakeholders is a failure to effectively manage the organization's capacity to generate future wealth.[10]

To measure long-term wealth creation, the system I envision quantifies and evaluates the internalization of social costs and practices of sustainability as well.

Valuing corporations' contributions to the public interest in this way complements the business case approach because it too applies in situations where short-term profits and long-term wealth coincide. It also works well with values-driven models because it encompasses situations when investing in long-term wealth coincides with societal norms and managers' personal values. Yet it avoids the limitations of the business case because it values wealth creation rather than short-term profits and moves decision making out to the long term. It also avoids the limitations of values-driven models by making the measurement and assessment of actual investments—rather than the assertion of general commitments—the basis for debate in the marketplace. In short, this model offers a means to bridge the gap between the worlds of pure profit and pure values.

Because this system is expressed through the marketplace, it also has the advantages of flexibility and innovation that come with the market's entrepreneurial spirit. This flexibility can play itself out on a national or cultural level. That is to say, although long-term wealth measurement may take as its basis the assessment of productivity, internalization of costs, sustainable management, and investments in stakeholder relations, it can express itself differently in different cultures. For example, some societies or segments of society may value most highly the preservation of the small and local, others will focus on improving opportunities for women and minorities, others will place greatest emphasis on involving employees in decision making, others will make the rights of animals a major concern, and still others will find that job creation is one of their primary expressions of value to community. A system of measurements allows a wide variety of achievements to be recognized, debated, and tailored to fit the particular cultures, histories, and needs of different communities without being narrowly prescriptive.

Because it relies on a well-ordered marketplace for its implementation, this system also has the virtue of forcing government to define its role. First, government must decide on the scope of the goods and services that can most appropriately and efficiently be delivered through the marketplace and distinguish them from those better provided by the public sector. Thus, government retains the responsibility for defining which tasks should be allocated to the markets and which should not. Second, this system depends on a strong governmental hand to establish transparency and integrity in the marketplace, because both full disclosure and absence of conflicts of interest are essential if this marketplace is to send credible, consistent signals to the business community on long-term wealth creation.

Such a system would allow government to avoid returning to many of the direct ownership and regulatory practices it has recently abandoned. But it has drawbacks as well. Chief among them is the considerable effort and expense necessary for its creation. Government must be willing and able to allocate the time and resources necessary to ensure a level playing field on which debates about the relative value created by corporations can take place. And investors, consumers, and other stakeholders must be persuaded that it is in their best interests to take an active and ongoing part in these debates. If government does not or cannot make the necessary investments, or if investors, consumers, and others ultimately do not wish to play an active role, then society runs a substantial risk of creating expectations that cannot be fulfilled. Inevitably the public will be disappointed if expectations that corporations will act in the public interest cannot be realized. Similarly, corporate managers will be frustrated if they receive no consistent feedback from society on what these public interests are. These disappointments and frustrations will in all likelihood lead to a volatile and unpredictable world of mutual distrust and recrimination between business and society, and should be avoided if at all possible.

The effort and expense involved in creating such a system are considerable, yet the system is not inconceivable or unachievable. Part 2 of this book discusses pioneering efforts that have been made to date to lay its foundation—efforts made in particular by those in the SRI and CSR communities—and what remains to be done to build an effective structure on this initial work. The first three chapters in part 2 are devoted to the three key initiatives: chapter 4 discusses the steps that need to be taken to ensure comprehensive disclosure of data on corporations' social and environmental records; chapter 5 looks at the steps that need to be taken to cultivate adequate, objective analysis and debate based on that data and their dissemination to a well-informed and financially sophisticated base of investors and consumers; and chapter 6 discusses how to create mechanisms that will allow investors and consumers, along with other stakeholders, to appropriately reward those companies with the most deserving records. The net effect of these three initiatives will be to transform today's marketplace into one better able to guide corporations toward a broadly conceived public interest. Chapter 7 then looks forward to the specific means at the disposal of government and the stakeholders in the corporation to realize this transformation.

PART TWO

Transforming the Marketplace

CHAPTER FOUR

The First Step:
Data and Disclosure

THE FIRST STEP IN BUILDING A TRANSPARENT MARKETPLACE IN
which the ability of corporations to generate long-term wealth may be
assessed is to make sure that the data needed for this assessment is available. As we will see, those in the socially responsible investing and corporate social responsibility movements have made progress over the
past three decades in identifying key positive and negative indicators to
quantify and assess corporations' externalization of costs, contributions to sustainability, and investments in stakeholder relations. The
challenge now is ensuring that companies disclose the data needed to
make consistent assessments of these activities.

Ensuring adequate disclosure is a substantial challenge, and my
experience in the field leads me to believe that four separate mechanisms will ultimately be required. First, in order to establish a baseline
of comparable data for multinational corporations, a global system of
voluntary disclosure, such as that developed by the Global Reporting
Initiative, described later in this chapter, will be crucial. Second,
national regulators will need to mandate disclosure of key data, as
French law already requires. Third, also at a national level, for specific
issues of overriding societal concern, there will need to be detailed disclosure of key data in disaggregated format. Since the early 1990s, for
example, banks and other lending institutions in the United States are
required by the Home Mortgage Disclosure Act to disclose their loans

by region and type in order to make sure that poorer neighborhoods are not victims of discrimination. Finally, companies will need to continue to be encouraged to tell their own stories in their own words so they can highlight their strongest or most innovative social and environmental initiatives.

This system of overlapping disclosure methods may sound elaborate, but it is necessary to accommodate the varying needs of both the financial markets and other stakeholders and their different approaches to valuing corporations.

How Disclosure Has Grown Since the 1970s

It is remarkable how little the general public knows about publicly traded corporations today. Regulators require voluminous financial data, but they have done little to help us understand the basics of how corporations affect daily life in other ways. We know a company's inventory turnover, its cost of goods sold, its interest expenses, and its accounts receivable. But we do not know its workplace safety records, its greenhouse gas emissions, its record on promotion of women and minorities, or the nature of its environmental policies and practices.

When the Council on Economic Priorities (CEP) began conducting its studies of corporate environmental and social records in the early 1970s, little CSR information was publicly available. Through substantial efforts, CEP obtained data directly from the companies themselves for its studies of the environmental records of the pulp and paper, steel, and electric utility industries. The level of cooperation varied from company to company and from industry to industry. Still, these studies broke new ground by bringing previously unavailable environmental and social data to the public's attention, and thereby making comparisons of companies in specific industries possible for the first time. In its 1972 study of the banking industry's record on women and minorities, CEP commented on its poor cooperation, noting that the "lack of cooperation underlines the fact that banks enjoy power without accountability. Information on bank employment and lending practices is virtually unobtainable from any source except the bank itself."[1] At that time, CEP called for more consistent and widespread public disclosure of such data, without which comprehensive comparisons across multiple issues for multiple companies were not possible.

By the time I began my SRI research work with KLD Research & Analytics (KLD) in 1990, there had been some progress on broad disclosure of social and environmental data for large publicly traded companies. In addition to the more traditional reports on charitable contributions, some corporate environmental and health and safety reports were beginning to appear. At a national level, reasonably comprehensive data on releases of toxic chemicals had just become available, as had increased data on bank lending practices. The number of community and environmental groups monitoring corporate activities at a local level had also grown, providing yet another source of information.

Today, the landscape continues to change, particularly in the area of voluntary corporate reporting. An ever-increasing number of companies, including many of the largest multinational corporations, now publish sustainability and environmental reports. Statistics compiled by the Corporate Register, a U.K.-based Web site that tracks corporate nonfinancial reporting around the world, show that over 1,900 such reports were published either in hard copy or electronically in 2003.[2] As of mid-2004, CSRwire, a U.S.-based corporate social responsibility Web site, posted links to some 355 CSR reports.[3] Organizations seeking to encourage such public reporting recognize the best of these as models. The U.K.-based Association of Chartered Certified Accountants, which began an awards program for sustainability, environmental, and social reporting by U.K. companies in 1991, is among the most prominent of such organizations. It has cosponsored a similar awards program in Europe since 1996, and since 2000 has partnered with others around the world to recognize superior reporting annually by companies in North America, Asia, South Asia, and South Africa.

Despite this progress, the kind of systematic and comprehensive data necessary to provide market forces with the ability to act on social and environmental records is still lacking. If markets are to be a driving force that encourages companies that make efforts to create long-term wealth and discourages those that don't, then the available data needs to be more systematic and comprehensive. Those advocating a strong role for markets in directing society to its desired ends, such as economist Friedrich von Hayek, believe that markets are efficient mechanisms for processing and acting on vast quantities of data, particularly at a local level—more efficient, they argue, than governments.[4] With good data in hand, markets can find flexible, innovative, experimental, and efficient solutions to complicated problems. The more data, the better.

As I noted in chapter 2, long-term wealth creation is tied closely to considerations of the stakeholders in the corporation. It is therefore not surprising that, as the SRI and CSR communities began to examine corporate records, they gathered and organized the data into categories relevant to stakeholders. For example, KLD's profiles of U.S. corporations are divided into seven basic categories: community, employees, diversity, product, corporate governance, human rights, and the environment. Similarly, the Sustainable Investment Research International Group (SiRi), an international coalition of SRI research firms, divides its corporate profiles into community, corporate governance, customers, employees, environment, human rights and supply chain, and controversial business activities.

KLD further characterizes the data it presents in each category as "strengths" and "concerns." In the area of the environment, for example, the strengths include beneficial products and services, clean energy, alternative fuels, pollution prevention, recycling, and communications.

The concerns include hazardous wastes, regulatory problems, climate change, ozone-depleting chemicals, agricultural chemicals, and substantial emissions. The SiRi Group organizes its data somewhat differently. In each stakeholder category, it begins with an assessment of the company's public reports and communications to each stakeholder group, following this with an assessment of its principles and policies and its management systems in the area. This assessment is then followed by details on key data, notable strengths, and notable concerns. These details provide a snapshot of the company's actual performance.

Other SRI research organizations offering similar profiles, such as CoreRatings, Innovest, and EIRIS (discussed further in the next chapters), vary somewhat in their formats and the data points on which they focus. CoreRatings stresses the element of risk assessment and targets its research to financial analysis. Innovest has a detailed quantitative scoring system. EIRIS packages the data it provides to allow its clients to screen companies by issue at varying levels of concern. Underlying these different emphases, however, is a similar focus on data that relates to the corporation's stakeholders.

Through this work, these research firms and advocates of CSR carrying out similar work over the past three decades have succeeded in identifying numerous indicators that measure the creation or destruction of long-term wealth. Much work remains to be done on quantifying and assessing the implications of these indicators, but a solid framework for evaluation has been established.

Ensuring Disclosure

Once the relevant stakeholders and pertinent data points are identified, how difficult is it to take the next steps to disclosure? In theory, the process appears straightforward. In practice, however, a number of complications arise. Among these are questions about whether disclosure should be mandatory or voluntary, globally harmonized or tailored to specific national and cultural concerns, provided as raw data points or as narration, aggregated on a company-wide level or broken out by local operations. There is also the question of whether the data disclosed should be targeted to the specific concerns of the financial community or the broader concerns of society in general.

The four approaches to disclosure described in the following paragraphs have emerged in recent years: international standards for disclosure, nationally mandated disclosure, disaggregated data, and voluntary individualized company disclosure. Each addresses these problems in a different way.

International Standards for Disclosure

Two organizations—the Coalition for Environmentally Responsible Economies (CERES) and the Global Reporting Initiative (GRI)—have made great strides toward creating the international expectation that corporations should voluntarily report social and environmental data in a thorough, consistent format.

The Coalition for Environmentally Responsible Economies (CERES)

CERES was created in 1988 in cooperation with the Social Investment Forum, the U.S. SRI trade association, under the leadership of Joan Bavaria of Trillium Asset Management (then known as Franklin Research and Development Corporation) and Denis Hayes of Earth Day (currently president of the Bullitt Foundation). Its creation was inspired by two pivotal events of that time: the environmental tragedy of the 1989 *Exxon Valdez* oil spill in Alaska and the success of the Sullivan principles in influencing the conduct of international corporations operating in South Africa. The former exemplified the lack of serious corporate concern for the environment; the latter, formally known as the Statement of Principles for South Africa, were a key element of the anti-apartheid movement and demonstrated how powerful publicly promulgated principles can be in highlighting issues of international concern and effecting change.

To pressure corporations to develop comprehensive environmental policies and practices, CERES developed a set of ten environmental principles, originally called the Valdez Principles, now called the CERES Principles. They addressed issues such as protection of the biosphere, sustainable use of natural resources, reduction of waste, energy conservation, and public communications. The tenth principle dealt with reporting itself, and it has become one of CERES's most important contributions to the SRI and CSR movements. Endorsing corporations must agree to the following:

> We will conduct an annual self-evaluation of our progress in implementing these principles. We will support the timely creation of generally accepted environmental audit procedures. We will annually complete the CERES report, which will be made available to the public.

CERES formed a multistakeholder advisory panel including representatives from the environmental, SRI, and corporate worlds to help its endorsing corporations report on environmental matters in a thorough and credible manner. This panel met regularly to define and refine its comprehensive environmental reporting format from the early 1990s through 1999. The resulting CERES reporting format was refined over the years until, by 1999, it contained ten sections with over a hundred data points on issues for which reporting was recommended. As of 2004, over seventy companies and organizations, primarily U.S.-based, had endorsed the CERES Principles.

The Global Reporting Initiative

In 1997 CERES began to explore ways to extend the principles it had developed for corporate environmental reporting to other social issues on a global scale. Under the leadership of Robert Massie, Jr., of CERES, and Allen White, of the Tellus Institute, the Global Reporting Initiative (GRI) evolved for several years as part of CERES. It was then spun off as a stand-alone organization in 2002. GRI's goal is to foster comparisons of the performance of corporations, across countries and industries, on a set of standardized metrics that have been developed through a multistakeholder process. GRI's work has done much to develop a global consensus on which social and environmental indicators should most appropriately become standards when corporations produce their reports. As part of this process, it works through a sixty-member stakeholder council of representatives from business, accounting, investment, environmental, human rights, research, and labor organizations. This council develops and maintains what are called the GRI Sustainability Reporting Guidelines.

These guidelines are the global, multi-issue equivalent of CERES's environmental report. They identify standards for economic, environmental, and social reporting, in keeping with the vocabulary of sustainability and "triple bottom line" investing. The economic indicators include data on customers, suppliers, employees, and providers of capital. The environmental indicators include data on materials usage, energy, water, biodiversity, emissions, suppliers, products, compliance, and transport. The social indicators fall into four categories: labor practices and decent work (employee relations, health and safety, training, diversity), human rights (nondiscrimination, unions, child and forced labor, disciplinary and security practices, indigenous peoples), society (community, bribery, political contributions, pricing), and product responsibility (customer safety, advertising, privacy).

In each category the guidelines have core and additional indicators. The 2002 version specified approximately forty-six core indicators and ninety-seven additional indicators.[5] A total of fifty-one of these core and additional indicators relate to environmental issues. As of September 2004, GRI reported that some 550 companies worldwide made reference to its indicators in their sustainability reporting.[6]

It is difficult to overstate the importance of CERES and GRI in setting the tone for corporate environmental and social reporting worldwide. CERES has broadened its focus to include the fiduciary implications of environmental issues, particularly relating to global warming, for corporations and their boards of directors. Now headquartered in Amsterdam, GRI has built bridges to the United Nations and its Global Compact, a code of corporate conduct that has gained widespread recognition. Together they have created a worldwide expectation that corporations have an obligation to society to report key data on their social and environmental policies and practices.

Despite their successes, these initiatives still face challenges. Because adoption of the GRI guidelines is voluntary, it can be difficult to persuade companies to take up this reporting format. For example, as of 2004, seven years after GRI first began its work, only about fifty of the several thousand publicly traded companies in the United States had adopted its guidelines in part. Furthermore, many adopters worldwide report on only a limited number of the core and additional indicators. GRI has defined what full compliance with its guidelines means ("in accordance" status), and is still working to determine how to encourage complete, rather than partial, compliance. As of September 2004, GRI reported that only about forty-two companies and organizations worldwide were reporting in full accordance.[7]

Actually implementing a worldwide voluntary reporting system is a daunting task. However, CERES and GRI have clearly established the need for disclosure of key social and environmental data points that cut across national boundaries and unite a variety of stakeholders in the modern corporation.

Nationally Mandated Disclosure

One obvious way to overcome the limits of voluntary international disclosure is to mandate disclosure at the national level. Several countries, most notably France, have taken steps in this direction. Chief among the strengths of this approach is that it compels reporting systematically. However, one fundamental question is whether that reporting should address only the needs of the financial community or those of other stakeholders as well.

With the passage of its New Economic Regulations Act in 2001, France became the first country to mandate systematic CSR reporting by publicly traded corporations. French regulators subsequently spelled out the specific social and environmental indicators on which companies are required to report, and actual reporting began in 2003. Approximately forty indicators cover environmental performance, community initiatives, and employee relations. Many of the indicators are similar to those specified under the GRI guidelines; others were taken from the *bilan social*—a social balance sheet that covers employee relations—that French companies were already required to provide. This initiative promises to make social and environmental data available for the first time to a marketplace in a detail and scope analogous to that for disclosure of financial data.

A review of the first year of reporting in 2003 was prepared by the French CSR consulting firm Utopies. It found mixed results. On the negative side, Utopies noted that some 20 of the 120 companies in the SBF 120 Index (the most commonly used benchmark index of large publicly traded companies in France) effectively did no reporting, and two-thirds reported on fewer than 40 percent of the required indicators. For at least one indicator—the social and environmental performance that companies expected of their vendors and subcontractors—only 9 percent reported. In addition, some companies chose, as they can legally do, to report only on their headquarters' operations.

In addition, the Utopies study found that the law had several immediate, positive effects. Reporting of at least some basic CSR data increased to 69 percent of major firms in 2003. Most major companies had appointed CSR managers. A market for CSR data had begun to emerge, and two CSR rating firms were in operation (CoreRatings France and Vigeo), along with consultants providing CSR services and auditing CSR performance. Academic programs focusing on CSR had sprung up and a class of journalists specializing in CSR had begun to cover the issues regularly in the financial press. Equally important, according to Utopies, there had been general acceptance of the concept of mandatory reporting in the corporate community.

The Utopies study went on to point out several weaknesses in the current scheme. The data points for which reporting is mandated are less relevant for certain industries—such as the financial sector, the media, and retail firms—than for others. At some firms, CSR budgets are consumed more in data collection than in implementation of new programs. The actual CSR reports often tend not to highlight material risks and are difficult to interpret. Furthermore, the regulations are unclear on what verification, if any, is required for the reported data. Regulations require companies to provide missing data if shareholders request it, and certain provisions exist for shareholders to sue if failure to disclose has harmed them. How meaningful these sanctions will be in practice is still unknown.[8]

In the United Kingdom, a different approach to the disclosure of social and environmental data is emerging, one that stresses its relevance to the financial markets. As part of a multiyear review and revision of the "Company Law" that governs all corporations in the country, a government-sponsored working group has established guidelines for corporate boards for complying with proposed legal obligations to disclose social and environmental data relevant to their operations. The working group's recommendations, issued in May 2004, specify among other things that the directors of a company be responsible for determining what social and environmental data is relevant and ensuring that it is appropriately reported.

This disclosure is to be made in the Operating and Financial Review (OFR) that management includes in its annual report to stockowners. The data is to be included when it is material to the business's operations. Or to put it differently, it is to be reported "to the extent necessary" for stockowners to evaluate the company's prospects for success. The recommendations specify that data on employees, the environment, and community is often relevant to a company's long-term success. It is therefore advised that in order to make informed decisions about what data to disclose, the board should develop sufficient skills and knowledge to evaluate these issues and consult with the key stakeholder groups that can affect the company's performance.[9]

In the United States, a number of advocates of CSR and SRI have raised similar questions about the materiality of social and environmental data in corporate public filings. (Information is generally deemed material if a reasonable investor would consider it significant in the total mix of information available to assess a company's prospects for success.) Since the 1970s, the Securities and Exchange Commission (SEC) has required U.S. corporations to disclose a limited amount of environmental data: estimated future costs for cleaning up hazardous waste sites and involvement in environmental lawsuits involving federal agencies that are likely to result in fines or penalties of over $100,000.[10] In July 2004, the Government Accountability Office issued a report in response to a request by members of Congress to determine if the SEC was adequately enforcing these environmental disclosure requirements. The report concluded: "Little is known about the extent to which companies are disclosing environmental information in their filings with the SEC," and "the adequacy of the SEC's efforts to monitor and enforce compliance with environmental disclosure requirements cannot be determined without more definitive information on the extent of environmental disclosure."[11]

As of mid-2004, those calling for increased environmental disclosure included a number of treasurers and comptrollers of states and cities in the United States, and eight of them had written the SEC to urge it to consider the issue of global warming as material to company operations. Similarly, in 2002, the Rose Foundation, an environmental foundation with a strong activist history, petitioned the SEC to require additional environmental disclosure on the grounds that it is material to stockowners, and in 2003 and 2004 it published studies of accounting loopholes that allow environmental liabilities to go unreported or be underreported.[12] In addition, the Corporate Sunshine Working Group, a coalition of U.S. environmental organizations and concerned investors coordinated by Michelle Chan-Fishel of Friends of the Earth, has urged that the SEC require companies to disclose additional social and environmental information in twenty different areas. The data identified relates in large part to liability risks the company might face in such areas as overseas bribery, product safety, union disputes, labor practices, allegations of discrimination, environmental controversies, and workplace safety.[13]

The virtue of the materiality approach is that it ties disclosure of social and environmental information to the already well-accepted principle that information should be disclosed when it helps shareholders evaluate a firm's financial prospects. The drawback to this approach is that it may prompt only sporadic disclosure of what companies judge to be material to their operations. Law professor Cynthia A. Williams, in an article in *Harvard Law Review*, argued that the SEC has the power to require social, as well as financial, disclosure. Williams points out that in the 1934 legislation creating the SEC, Congress empowered it to require disclosure in corporate proxy statements "as necessary or appropriate in the public interest or for the protection of investors."[14]

The public interest here could be interpreted to encompass corporations' social and environmental records.

Disaggregated Data

If the goal is long-term wealth creation, and not simply assessment of potential corporate profitability, then disaggregated data is also crucial. By *disaggregated data,* I mean data that documents the specific records of local corporate operations: the environmental records of the oil refineries in a particular community, the lending records of a bank in a low-income neighborhood, the safety record of a local steel plant, the records of promotions of women and minorities in the apparel industry, the workplace conditions at the overseas contractors from which a company sources, or the precise nature of military contracting.

Disaggregated data can be a crucial resource for those who advocate change in company policies or who wish to praise individual company initiatives. Such information can empower stakeholders other than stockowners in their dialogues with corporations. For example, CERES and the Tellus Institute, the original forces behind the GRI, have launched the Facility Reporting Project, which issued its first draft guidelines for voluntary facility reporting by corporations in June 2004. One of its goals is to "empower community organizations in interaction with individual facilities."[15]

Moreover, disaggregated data in raw form can provide a useful check on the accuracy of aggregated reporting. Corporations may be inclined to stress the positives and downplay the negatives in the process of aggregation. But if they disclose the raw data, employees, communities, and customers can understand what is happening on local levels and independent research groups can conduct analyses and reach their own conclusions.

Requiring disclosure of disaggregated data has two primary drawbacks. First, legislative processes are often necessary to force this disclosure. This process can be complicated and hard-fought, with corporations exercising considerable influence. Second, the amount of data generated can be voluminous and often confusing. Despite these challenges, it is of great value to society when companies disclose disaggregated data on certain issues. Two examples of useful disaggregated data that is already available in the United States are the Toxics Release Inventory, which annually provides details on industrial chemical emissions, and the Home Mortgage Disclosure Act, which provides details on bank lending patterns.

The Toxics Release Inventory (TRI)

The TRI provides relatively comprehensive and consistent data on the releases and recycling of toxic chemicals by major U.S. corporations. The first step toward disclosure of this data was taken in 1986 with the passage of the Emergency Planning and Community Right-to-Know Act, which passed in the wake of the 1984 explosion of a Union Carbide chemical plant in Bhopal, India, and subsequent, though less serious, releases in West Virginia. This legislation requires companies to disclose, at the plant level, the quantities of toxic chemicals stored and released. Disclosure of releases is made to the Toxics Release Inventory database, maintained by the U.S. Environmental Protection Agency (EPA). The TRI's purpose, according to the EPA, is "to empower citizens, through information, to hold companies and local governments accountable in terms of how toxic chemicals are managed."[16]

The disclosures required under the TRI have been expanded several times in the years since its creation. In 1990, the Pollution Prevention Act required additional disclosure of data on recycling, use reduction, and disposal of toxic chemicals, with the goal of encouraging reduced use of toxic chemicals. In 1998 the number of industries required to report was expanded by seven, including the electric utilities, metals mining, and coal mining industries, among others. Over the years, the number of chemicals on which reporting is required has also increased steadily from just over 300 originally to approximately 650 as of 2004. TRI has become an international model for such reporting, prompting similar initiatives in other countries such as Canada, Mexico, and Japan.

When the TRI data was first released to the public in the late 1980s, it provoked a tremendous reaction. Newspapers listed the top emitters of toxics countrywide. Local papers published specific figures on the largest polluters in their region. Although the releases reported were legal, pressure built rapidly for companies to monitor and reduce their emissions. In 1988 the EPA launched its "33/50" program that called for voluntary 50 percent reductions in corporate releases and transfers of seventeen particularly toxic chemicals by 1995. In 1995 the EPA reported that releases and transfers of these chemicals had been reduced by 55 percent nationwide.[17] To serve the needs of grassroots environmental organizations, online computer access to this data has been developed by nonprofit organizations such as RTK NET (the Right-to-Know Network, described further in the next chapter) and Environmental Defense.

The Home Mortgage Disclosure Act (HMDA)

Similarly specific disaggregated data on bank lending in economically disadvantaged neighborhoods has empowered activists in their ongoing campaigns to increase access to capital among low-income neighborhoods. In the 1970s, Congress passed the Home Mortgage Disclosure Act (HMDA) and the Community Reinvestment Act (CRA) to help address "redlining"—that is, bank policies of not lending in low-income neighborhoods from which they draw deposits. However, the amount of data disclosed under HMDA proved to be inadequate for meaningful monitoring of bank lending. In 1989, when Congress passed the Financial Institutions Reform,

Recovery and Enforcement Act (FIRREA) to address the crisis in the savings and loan industry of that time, an additional requirement was included that greatly expanded the amount of disclosure on lending for single-family and multifamily housing. The data provided details on the income levels and racial mix of those to whom loans were made. In 1995 CRA regulations were further expanded to include reports on lending to small businesses and farms.

In the hands of community activists, church groups, and others concerned about access to capital in low- and moderate-income neighborhoods, the HMDA data has proven to be an effective tool in bringing about improvements in bank lending programs over the past fifteen years. The CRA also handed these activists a particularly powerful tool when it permitted federal regulators to block mergers of banks if their records on community reinvestment proved to be inadequate. The public availability of specific, community-based data on lending has made it possible for community organizations to document their concerns about banks' lending records and extract concessions from these powerful financial institutions at the crucial moment when mergers are taking place.

Detailed disclosure at this level empowers stakeholders to evaluate companies' wealth-creating records and to push for specific improvements based on fact. However, the amount of data generated is staggering. Under HMDA for 2002, for example, 7,771 financial institutions reported on approximately thirty million loans. The TRI database contains a similarly overwhelming number of data points. In addition, disclosing the data is a time-consuming and costly task for corporations, and maintaining the resulting databases a substantial commitment for the government agencies to which this disclosure is made. For these reasons, it is likely that only a limited number of data points can be targeted for disclosure on a disaggregated level. Careful consideration should be given to those of greatest urgency.

Voluntary Individualized Company Disclosure

As previously noted, a number of corporations are already engaging in CSR disclosure voluntarily, and this is encouraging. That these reports are varied and idiosyncratic may be equally encouraging. Individualized reports give corporations an opportunity to tell their story in ways that highlight their particular strengths and innovations, address their particular controversies, and are tailored to their different stakeholders' varying concerns.

Two Canadian companies with strong commitments to CSR illustrate the range of approaches now being taken. Suncor Energy, a dominant player in the Canadian oil and natural gas industry, is among the most thorough implementers of reporting in accordance with GRI guidelines. In 2003 it published a seventy-eight-page sustainability report, separate from its financial reports, that was organized by social, environmental, and economic performance. It included more than fifteen pages of audited, yearly performance indicators (that is, specific CSR data points) for the most recent five years. As GRI requires, the report contained a GRI Content Index that allowed readers to readily identify where in the text GRI reporting requirements were addressed. Moreover, the report took time to address in detail issues with particular relevance to Canada, such as aboriginal relations.[18]

Dofasco, a leading Canadian steel producer, has taken a contrasting approach. It included its CSR reporting along with the financial statements in its annual report to shareholders in 2002. It organized this reporting by stakeholder (customers, employees, communities, suppliers), used the language of wealth generation, and provided data on a limited number of initiatives that it believes are the most important. A section titled "Social Well-Being: Prosperity" reported on contributions to profit sharing, taxes paid, and local purchases. In "Social Well-Being: Quality of Life," it reported on its health and safety record, expenditures on employee education, and levels of employee satisfaction. In its environmental section, it highlighted data on benzene and particulate emissions and discharges of pollutants to Hamilton Harbor.[19]

A third approach is taken by the U.S. medical products firm Baxter International, which has tied its environmental indicators more explicitly to financial performance. The company aggregates and quantifies its cost savings from environmental management programs each year. Its sustainability report contains an "Environmental Financial Statement" detailing its "environmental costs" and "environmental savings." In 2002, it reported that its total income, savings, and cost-avoidance for environmental initiatives were approximately $65 million, up from $60 million the previous year.[20]

These different approaches to reporting reflect the differing views companies have on how best to convey the particular strengths of their CSR initiatives.

Recent developments at the Body Shop, a company with long experience in CSR reporting, are instructive as to why a company may consider it important to supplement standardized and mandatory reporting with individualized and voluntary initiatives. Founded in 1976 by Anita Roddick, the Body Shop soon became a leading proponent of corporate social responsibility, tying its brand name and image to forward-looking policies on the environment, animal testing, employees, and community involvement. After questions arose in the early 1990s over whether it was living up to its claims and "walking the talk," the company issued CSR reports in 1995 and 1997. These reports covered the range of CSR and sustainability indicators that have since become part of comprehensive disclosure. Its 1997 report, for example, was over 200 pages long.

In the five years following 1997, the company underwent a difficult financial period during which it issued no CSR reports. In 2003 it began reporting again, but took a new tack. Instead of issuing a single comprehensive CSR report, it began publishing a series of reports targeted to specific stakeholder groups. Explaining this new approach, the company wrote:

> We believe the future lies in more personal and targeted communications that respond to the current interests and information needs of our stakeholders. Our reporting approach is evolving from being information-driven to performance-led. By this, we mean that we are moving away from a "broad-brush" approach providing detailed information across an array of issues. Instead, we want to present an account of the key impacts, risks, and issues that are of relevance and priority to our business, our sector, and our stakeholders today.[21]

Thus in 2003 the Body Shop published reports tailored to the concerns of employees, shareholders, and environmentalists, as well as a separate report on community giving. In the first half of 2004, the company added a suppliers report and plans a report on franchisees. The company maintains a report "library" on its Web site, where those interested can view its policy documents, codes of conduct, and principles. The Web site also has specific sections devoted to issues on which the company has taken particularly public stances, such as animal testing, self-esteem (that is, its representation of women in advertising), and community trade (that is, its sourcing of natural products in developing countries at fair prices).

Because it is flexible, the Body Shop's new approach addresses several problems inherent in CSR reporting. One set of stakeholders often has little interest in issues of paramount importance to another. For an animal rights advocate, other issues may be secondary. Tailoring its CSR reports to specific stakeholders facilitates such communications. In addition, the data points on which standardized reporting formats tend to rely can miss crucial elements of a company's story, which is better conveyed in narratives tailored to management's thinking and the company's particular efforts. Finally, comprehensive CSR reports can make daunting, and even boring, reading. In contrast, targeted reports can convey the essence of a company's efforts on its most important initiatives in ways that bring the issues to life. Detailed backup materials that satisfy the needs of specialists can then be reported separately.

A Need for All Four Approaches

It may seem excessive to suggest that all four reporting formats described in this chapter are necessary to make CSR data useful to society, but I believe that no one approach can accomplish the complicated challenges inherent in the process. Companies frequently complain about the time and effort required for reporting; they talk about suffering from "survey fatigue." But the variety of needs that these data must meet necessitates this complexity. The various stakeholders for whom this data is of use have differing goals and concerns, relate to the corporation in different ways, and are located in different parts or regions of the world. Nothing less than varied and comprehensive avenues for data disclosure will accommodate their needs and allow them to communicate their concerns.

CHAPTER FIVE

The Second Step:
Analysis and Debate

DISCLOSING SOCIAL AND ENVIRONMENTAL DATA IS THE FIRST
step on the road to assessing when and how corporations act in the public interest, but the data alone does not tell the whole story. It must be
processed and analyzed, compared and contrasted, disseminated and
debated.

The first part of this chapter looks at the challenges involved in
the analysis of issue-specific and industry-specific data, the compilation
of overall company records, and the comparison of companies' performance in their industries. Meeting these challenges requires the
work of research organizations that I call *infomediaries* and *raters*, respectively. The second half of the chapter discusses the cultural change that
will be necessary if the public is to understand and debate these analyses
and comparisons. Bringing about this cultural change will require,
among other things, demystifying the language that surrounds the business and financial communities and debating the concepts fundamental
to these communities, such as return on investment, price, and corporate citizenship. As we will see, the experiences of the socially responsible investing and corporate social responsibility movements illustrate
the potential for progress in both areas.

Processing and Rating the Data

As was noted in chapter 4, increasing amounts of data are available to researchers who assess corporate social and environmental per-

formance. This is both a positive development—because tools for measuring actual performance are more and more at hand—and a challenge—because understanding the significance of voluminous data is time-consuming and costly. Thirty years ago, the problem was too little data. Five years from now, the problem may be too much.

To process and assess the data, two different but related types of research organizations are needed. The first type, which I call an *infomediary organization*,[1] takes issue-specific or industry-specific information, compiles it, processes it, and interprets it. These organizations have the specialized knowledge that is often needed to deal with specialized data. The work of an infomediary organization is much like that of a scientific research institute, which understands complex scientific subjects, such as genetic engineering, for example, and then helps pharmaceutical industry analysts understand which companies' new technologies are likely to succeed. The second type of organization, which I call a *rating agency*, assembles processed data and compiles an overall picture—including both the positives and the negatives—of a company's record. Rating agencies provide the valuable service of distilling information on numerous issues, distinguishing the relevant from the irrelevant; they also weigh the often-conflicting records of a single company. This presentation of positives and negatives in a manner that is reasonable and fair is important for the debate about corporations' ability to create long-term wealth and act in the public interest. The role of rating agencies resembles that of industry analysts in the mainstream financial community, who compile and analyze diverse information about a company to predict stock performance; the same kind of quantitative skills and judgment based on experience are needed to assess a company's overall wealth-creating contributions to society.

Infomediaries

To better understand the challenges that processing specialized data present, let us examine more closely the task of working with the

Toxics Release Inventory (TRI) data, described in chapter 4. As noted, many U.S. companies are required to report their use of toxic chemicals when it exceeds certain thresholds. They file this data with the Environmental Protection Agency (EPA), by chemical and by facility. The resulting material, including millions of points of raw data, is rich but confusing and difficult for the uninitiated to make sense of.

The TRI data is complex for many reasons. At the simplest level, it is difficult to compile because chemicals can be listed under differing names, as can the parent companies of the reporting facilities. Mergers and acquisitions also mean that facilities reported under one company name one year need to be compiled under another company name the next.

Once sorted by company and by chemical category, the reported data must then be carefully interpreted. The data provided for a single chemical distinguishes among intentional discharges directly to the air, water, and land; transfers to off-site waste treatment facilities; on-site treatment; recycling or burning on-site and off-site; and accidental one-time releases. The same chemical released into the water might cause harm, but it might be essentially benign when released into the air. Because chemicals differ in their relative toxicity, the release of ten pounds of one chemical may be far more serious than ten pounds of another. Moreover, the toxicity of a chemical itself—for example, whether it is a carcinogen or not, and if so, in what concentrations—can be the subject of scientific debate. Analyses must be flexible enough to reflect these varying factors.

Determining the appropriate industry peers with which to compare a company's record presents another challenge. In the pulp and paper industry, for example, there are three distinct business lines, each with its own production processes and environmental issues. The management of forests for harvesting timber and of mills to produce lumber generates few toxic chemicals to be reported, although use of herbicides and pesticides is an issue. The pulping and bleaching processes that convert logs into paper products use numerous toxic chemicals. The adhesives used by the building products industry in plywood, veneer, particleboard, and similar products generate yet another set of environmental challenges. To compare one company's toxic releases to those of another, an analyst needs to account for the relative percentages of these three business lines in their operations.

Finally, it is not always clear why reported reductions or increases in toxic chemicals have occurred. A reduction one year may have been caused by improved environmental management, but it may equally well have come about because production was lower that year or a subsidiary was divested. To complicate the task of analysis further, the number and types of chemicals on which reporting is required under TRI can change from year to year.

RTK Net

When data from the TRI started to become available to the general public in the late 1980s, its size and complexity made it difficult to use. One of the first organizations to address the challenge was the Right-to-Know Network, known as RTK NET. RTK NET is a project of OMB Watch, a Washington, D.C.–based nonprofit research and advocacy organization that promotes citizen participation and government accountability. In 1990 OMB decided to create RTK NET specifically to help community organizations use the TRI data.

RTK NET facilitates a variety of uses of the data reported through the TRI by assembling it into a database that is available free of charge over the Internet. Users can search this database by geographic region to obtain a picture of toxic chemicals used, released, or treated locally. They can find historical data for a single facility or for a parent company, if they want to track increases or decreases over time. They can compare the performance of different companies by assembling industry-wide data. Searches can also be run to track use of specific chemicals. The RTK NET system is set up to deliver reports at four increasingly detailed levels—summary, low, medium, and high—to accommodate differing levels of interest.

RTK NET provides background for database users, too: a history of TRI reporting, a discussion of technical terms, an assessment of its limitations, links to resources on the toxicity of specific chemicals, technical support for those using its database, and training. RTK NET also highlights the multiple interrelated uses that TRI data can serve, including educating the public about environmental problems, organizing communities, demonstrating environmental injustice, negotiating with corporations, influencing legislation, enforcing regulations, preventing pollution, preparing for emergencies, and improving business practices. RTK NET estimates that approximately 250,000 searches of the TRI data on its Web site are conducted by both individuals and organizations each year.

The group points to particular actions that access to its database has made possible. For example, Citizens for a Better Environment in Chicago and the North Baton Rouge Environmental Association in Louisiana documented the disproportionate exposure of low-income communities to cancer-causing chemicals in their states. The community organization PODER in Austin, Texas, forced companies to eliminate the potential for deadly accidents from stored hazardous wastes in low-income communities. The Paper Task Force convened by the public interest law firm Environmental Defense used the data to help reform environmental practices in the pulp and paper industry and currently hosts on its Web site a service called Scorecard, which allows communities to research local chemical releases. RTK Net has also been a valuable resource to the SRI research and investment communities in compiling analyses of corporations' environmental records over the years.[2]

CANICCOR and the Woodstock Institute

Infomediaries also do important work with the voluminous data made available by banks through the Home Mortgage Disclosure Act (HMDA). This data presents many of the same challenges in compilation and interpretation as the TRI data. Research organizations skilled at working with the millions of HMDA data points reported by lending institutions to their regulators each year have facilitated their use by the investment world and community groups. Two nonprofit organizations providing this service in different ways are CANICCOR and the Woodstock Institute.

Since the early 1990s, CANICCOR's analyses of HMDA data have been a valuable resource to the social investment community in the United States. Originally founded by church groups in the 1970s, CANICCOR early on helped concerned investors in their discussions with banks about international lending. As the more detailed HMDA data became available, CANICCOR, under the leadership of John Lind, began to analyze banks' domestic lending in low-income neighborhoods and to minorities. Over the years, these analyses have provided churches and other SRI investors a basis on which to enter negotiations with the likes of Bank of America, JPMorgan Chase, and Washington Mutual to increase their lending commitments to communities in need. Today CANICCOR numbers among its clients the Presbyterian, Lutheran, and Methodist churches, as well as SRI research and investment firms such as KLD Research & Analytics and Walden Asset Management.

The Woodstock Institute in Chicago takes a different, but equally effective, approach to HMDA data. Woodstock was founded in Chicago in the early 1970s to help low-income and minority communities gain access to credit and capital. Over the years, it has worked locally to empower community development organizations in their quest for economic self-sufficiency. Woodstock annually publishes its

Community Lending Fact Book, which reports on each bank's local lending patterns. These analyses, compiled from HMDA data, provide important support to community groups in their dialogues with local banks. Woodstock also provides technical assistance to community organizations wishing to interpret and use the data in their dealings with the banking community.

Because TRI and HMDA are rich and complicated data sets, intermediary analysis is essential to assure their usefulness. Other data sets currently available require similar compilation and interpretation. For example, the U.S. Department of Defense (DoD) annually publishes details on nonclassified contracts over $25,000. This data is helpful to those in the SRI community tracking weapons-related and nuclear weapons–related work by corporations. But the data published by the DoD often requires compilation and interpretation to be usable. Limited data sets are also available through other agencies, such as the Occupational Safety and Health Administration (providing data on workplace safety inspections) and the National Labor Relations Board (providing data on disputes between companies and unions). Each data set comes with its own complications and challenges. The Baltimore-based nonprofit organization Nuclear Free America is an example of an infomediary working with Department of Defense contracting data, particularly as it relates to companies involved in nuclear weapons contracting. Unions have been among the organizations most interested in analysis of OSHA's data, although they have also argued for more complete and specific disclosure.[3]

The Business & Human Rights Resource Centre

Another model of the infomediary organization is the Business & Human Rights Resource Centre, an independent London-based organization working in partnership with Amnesty International Business Groups and various academic institutions around the world. It is headed by Christopher Avery and maintains a Web site on which it assembles information on corporations and human rights issues.[4] As of 2004, this Web site provided access at no charge to articles and reports—both positive and negative—on human rights issues in general and on those relating specifically to some sixteen hundred companies around the world. As of July 2004, it reported receiving over forty-seven thousand visits per month. As with other specialized, controversial issues, the amount of data generated on human rights is vast and difficult to access without a provider of intermediary services.

The Future of Infomediaries

The availability of data on corporate social and environmental issues that exists today is only a precursor of what is to come. To cite just one example, as chapter 4 explained, the Global Reporting Initiative requests data on fifty-one core and additional indicators in the environmental area alone. Among these environmental indicators are four on disclosure of water usage. Water is likely to be an issue of increasing importance in the twenty-first century, and it will take specialized knowledge to interpret company-specific water usage data. Water usage issues are different for electric utilities, which use water for cooling; pulp and paper firms, which use it in manufacturing processes; beverage companies, which process it for consumption; and agribusinesses, which draw it from widely used aquifers and river basins.

For each SRI money manager and rating agency to develop its own in-house expertise on the intricacies of compiling and analyzing these data sets would be inefficient and expensive. Relying on specialized research firms for such analyses is a logical solution to this problem. Because of the volume of data that will become available in the coming years, a network of infomediary research shops will be of great use, specializing in such areas as water usage, ethics programs, greenhouse gas emissions, employment of the disabled, energy conservation, marketing issues, charitable giving, and so on.

The need for these research specialists may be clear, but it is less clear how they will be funded. The SRI world does not yet have the resources to pay the full cost of such research. Consequently, only a handful of infomediaries currently exist. Over time a market for their research can be cultivated, including clients in the SRI world, regulators, nonprofit and community organizations, and corporations themselves. Today, a kind of catch-22 prevents this market from developing: development of demand is hampered by a scarcity of providers and development of providers is hampered by a scarcity of demand. In other highly specialized fields, such as biotechnology, computer science, demographics, or consumer trends, similar infomediary-type organizations find diverse sources of funding from financial analysts, industry-related market researchers, funders of pure research, and governmental agencies, among others. Until a similarly diverse clientele can be cultivated for infomediaries specializing in corporate-related social and environmental data, these organizations will remain understaffed and underfunded.

The funding challenge is exacerbated by the need for these intermediaries to be independent, and thus credible. Their analyses will serve as the foundation for SRI ratings and therefore need to be trustworthy beyond doubt, so others can build on it. This complicates their ability to accept consulting contracts or funding from the corporations whose data they are analyzing, thereby eliminating a potentially lucrative source of income.

In the United States, one possible solution to this funding problem might be to allocate a portion of the millions of dollars in fines or penalties paid by corporations each year in financial scandals to endow a foundation dedicated to the cultivation of these niche-market research firms. Whatever the solution, it should be implemented with speed. Without a network of such specialized research firms, there is a risk of assuring the disclosure of social and environmental data, but not a capacity to analyze it.

Rating Agencies

Investors and other stakeholders wishing to interact with corporations usually start with an overview of their records and key data on their social and environmental records. A compilation of a broad range of data in a single place, particularly if it lays out the facts on controversial issues and provides some interpretation, can be valuable. It can save time, assure reasonable completeness, highlight relevant information, facilitate comparisons, provide materials for communications with corporate management, and inform debate on complicated issues.

Organizations that provide these compilations and comparisons are what I call *rating agencies*. As increasing amounts of data about corporations' social and environmental records become available in ever greater complexity, raters will become more essential. Their particular expertise grows from a familiarity with a broad range of issues, an ability to weigh the relative strengths and weaknesses of a company's record, a knowledge of the reliability of various information sources, an understanding of corporate cultures or themes that cut across issues, and a historical sense of trends in issues or industries or at individual firms.

Rating agencies rely on a wide variety of sources for their research, including infomediaries, government sources, the press, critics of the corporate world, stakeholders of the corporation, and corporations themselves. Their ability to evaluate independently and fairly is key to their credibility. The number of rating agencies has grown steadily since the mid-1990s. Most countries with developed stock markets now have at least one such active group. Large financial institutions, particularly in Europe and the United Kingdom, have also developed their own "green teams" to serve internal purposes and private clients.

The emergence of this network is a sign of progress. Because there is a growing market for such services in the financial community, these rating agencies have been able to tap resources that have allowed their growth and development. But a number of challenges remain. There are questions of how to develop greater resources to allow for work of greater depth, how to construct metrics and rating methodologies to allow for more sophisticated analysis, how to maintain the independence that is necessary for credibility, and how to make findings available outside the financial community for broader public debate. A review of the approaches taken by some of these firms helps illustrate both the challenges and the progress that has been made in meeting them. It should be noted that the limited number of SRI research operations mentioned here—including KLD Research & Analytics where I directed research for more than a decade—represents only a small sample of the numerous initiatives under way.

KLD Research & Analytics, Inc.

In 1990, I joined Peter Kinder and Amy Domini to found KLD Research & Analytics, Inc. (Kinder, Lydenberg, Domini & Co., at that time). One of our initial goals was to publish systematic research on the social and environmental records of publicly traded U.S. corporations. In our view, the absence of a comprehensive source of such research at that time was a substantial barrier to the growth of SRI in the investment community. We set out to develop a consistent methodology for analysis and to compile profiles on all companies in the Standard & Poor's 500 Index and the Domini 400 Social Index that we maintained. These profiles were ultimately published in an online database called *Socrates*, which continues to be marketed to the financial community today.

Rather than assigning companies an overall score or grade on their social and environmental records, KLD initially developed a system of indicators of "strengths" and "concerns." If a company passed thresholds on indicators related to the environment, employee relations, community, diversity, and other social areas, it received a strength or a concern rating. (Some sixty such positive and negative indicators were developed.) A company could have as many strengths or concerns as its record warranted, or none at all. This meant that countervailing strengths and concerns might coexist on the same issue. Reconciling conflicting indicators was less of a goal than providing an overall portrait of a company in all its complexity. The accompanying text, often quite extensive—KLD's longer profiles nowadays are over thirty pages—provide background text explaining a company's strengths or concerns, and additional information on other issues as well that might not trigger a rating.

Because these reports present clients with often complex profiles rather than a single, simple score, they are flexible in their use. SRI investors with different levels of concern about different issues are free to weigh each separately. KLD's data allows users to assess the appropriateness of its interpretation and completeness. Pro's and con's are laid out side by side and can be compared.

In many cases, the absence of an overall score does not pose problems for a user. A profile such as that of Green Mountain Coffee Roasters, Inc., the Vermont-based coffee firm, which describes seven strengths and no concerns, tells a straightforward story appealing to social investors. Similarly clear is the case of WGL Holdings, Inc., a natural gas distribution company based in Washington, D.C., which has six strengths and no concerns, or that of the large beauty products company Avon Products, with nine strengths and only two concerns. Similarly, when the report is overwhelmingly negative, a rating adds little value. For example, when the profile of a firm such as Reynolds American (formerly R.J. Reynolds Tobacco Holdings) has ten concerns (in addition to its involvement in tobacco) and only two strengths, a score or grade would add little to the story.[5]

More often, however, KLD profiles portray companies with a

mix of strengths and concerns. As of July 2004, the report on the U.S. pharmaceutical company Merck, for example, listed eight strengths and eight concerns, with an accompanying text profile that runs some thirty pages. The report revealed a company that has long had a reputation for integrity in the pharmaceutical industry, is historically a leader in research and development, is often cited among the best workplaces in America with a strong benefits program, and promotes women to top management positions and balances issues of work and family. The profile also noted a series of safety, marketing, and antitrust controversies, many relating to Merck's Medco subsidiary, which the company spun off in late 2003, disputes with the IRS over taxes owed, substantial environmental cleanup liabilities, and high levels of compensation for its CEO and board of directors. The profile also offered both praise and criticism for its programs to give away drugs to those in need and to address the question of affordability of drugs for HIV/AIDS.[6]

The situation was further complicated in September 2004 as this book was going to press when Merck voluntarily withdrew its drug Vioxx from the market for safety reasons amid controversies over when it first knew of these concerns. Evaluating a company's record—determining where it creates value for society and where it imposes costs—is no simple matter and subject to multiple interpretations.

KLD's initial approach has proven unusual in the world of SRI research. Most rating agencies provide numerical or letter grades for the companies they profile, either on specific issues, or on a company's overall performance, or on both. Clients appreciate the ease of use that these ratings and rankings bring. To accommodate that demand, KLD has developed a system for ranking companies within their industry. As of the writing of this volume, KLD plans to introduce more elaborate scoring and rating schemes, but remains committed to maintaining the wealth of data and the flexibility that its profiling has provided.

Michael Jantzi Research Associates, Inc.

In Canada, Michael Jantzi Research Associates, Inc. (MJRA), the leading SRI research provider in that country, takes an approach in profiling social and environmental records that is in many ways similar to KLD's. The firm highlights the companies' strengths and concerns in its profiles, backing them up with a wealth of detail, but it also scores the companies' overall performance and ranks them relative to their peers. The MJRA Canadian Social Investment Database contains profiles of some 250 Canadian firms. The firm also provides customized research services to meet the social and environmental concerns of individual clients.

Innovest Strategic Value Advisors

The international SRI research firm Innovest Strategic Value Advisors has adopted a research methodology that stresses ratings and rankings, tying these to questions of financial performance. Founded in 1995, Innovest's research first focused on the environmental policies and records of publicly traded companies but subsequently expanded to include other social indicators. Its company profiles include scores and ratings on environmental and social performance and relative rankings in their industries. The firm targets the financial community with its research, which it asserts can "uncover hidden value for potential investors."[7] It also suggests that "outperformers" on environmental and social issues are likely to be outperformers in the financial markets.

A June 2002 Innovest study, for example, assessed the environmental records of twenty-eight publicly traded electric utility companies, each ranked according to its overall score. Backtests of the performance of the companies with better-than-average scores showed that, as a group, their total shareholder returns substantially exceeded the returns of those with the lower scores over the prior three years. The report went on to note that historically the electric utilities "have not

been held accountable" for their negative impacts on public health and
the environment and that this externalization of costs "hides the real
cost of power for consumers." It asserted that environmental performance "will likely be a key determinate of [future] success." To its top scoring company, FPL Group, Inc., Innovest assigned a "AAA" rating and an
"outperform" status.[8] Innovest has done similar environmental sector
reports on the automobile, chemicals, forest products, oil and gas, phar-
maceuticals, semiconductors, and textile industries, among others.

Innovest calls its company profiles on other social indicators
"Intangible Value Assessments" or IVAs. Pointing out that stock prices
are increasingly driven by "intangible value drivers related to sustainability" that are not identified by traditional equity analysts, it scores
companies on their sustainable governance, human capital, stakeholder
capital, products/services, and emerging markets records. Under stakeholder capital, for example, Innovest scores companies on regulatory/
stakeholder relations, communities, and supply chain, and compares
these scores to those of the company's industry peers. It then assigns
the company an overall rating ranging from AAA to CCC. Its IVA for the
Canadian aluminum company Alcan, for example, gave the firm a number one ranking in its industry and a rating of AAA. The accompanying
profile provided basic data, as well as the scores, for each of these intangible asset drivers.[9]

CoreRatings

A similar ratings approach is taken by CoreRatings, headquartered in London. Until October 2004, CoreRatings was majority-
owned by Fimalac, the parent company of Fitch Ratings, one of the
three primary credit-rating services. At that time, it was acquired by Det
Norske Veritas (DNV), a Norwegian provider of risk management and
certification services. DNV's mission is "safeguarding life, property, and
the environment." Among other services, it provides certification for

corporations for the ISO 9000 quality standards, the ISO 14000 environmental standards, and the SA 8000 labor standards.

CoreRatings emphasizes the connection between social and environmental issues and financial risk. It begins this research with an assessment of the social, environmental, employment, corporate governance, and ethical risks for the industry sector in which a company operates. It then analyzes the investment implications of these risks and the adequacy of a company's management systems for coping with them. It conducts primary and secondary research—that is, it makes direct contact with the company and reviews publicly available information on its practices. Ultimately it gives the firm a grade, which can run from A+ to D. CoreRatings' risk factors are organized by stakeholder.

In addition, this firm provides a more confidential rating service to companies wishing to obtain an in-depth rating of themselves. The business model for this service is similar to that of credit-rating providers in that these ratings and reports are paid for by the firms. For this service, CoreRatings relies on communications with firms, including on-site visits, interviews with internal sources, and access to confidential information. Management can use the report and rating as an internal risk management tool and veto public disclosure of the ratings.

The Future of Rating Agencies

I have highlighted these efforts by raters to illustrate how far the SRI community has come in developing credible and varied rating systems. These examples also highlight a number of tensions that already exist in the rating process or may arise as it becomes more widely used.

The first tension is between providing research to the financial community, which can afford fees that are commensurate with the costs of doing the research but tends to make relatively narrow use of it, and providing it to other stakeholders—consumers, employees, communities—who may not be able to afford it but would make broader use of it. Rating agencies sometimes share their analyses with those in the non-profit community, but the tendency is to build business models on the financial community.

The second tension is between the ratings themselves and the data that supports them. The virtue of ratings and rankings is that they give the end user an immediate answer to the question of which companies are doing well or poorly. The backup data, however, provides the basis for informed debate. The ease of use that precise ratings and rankings provide may have two unintended consequences. First, because ratings are so convenient, they may discourage users from examining the underlying data, which can tell a story of complications and ambiguities. Second, if ratings are tied too closely to financial performance, there then is the risk of completely foregoing debates about larger, non-financial questions of the corporations' role in long-term wealth creation. In other words, if SRI research simply becomes one more tool for picking stocks, then much of its usefulness to society will be lost. The backup data's usefulness in generating debate should not be short-circuited by the ratings' ease of use.

Finally, as such ratings become more widely accepted and valued by corporations themselves, the independence of these rating agencies from the companies they rate will be increasingly important. The appearance of conflicts of interest might arise if rating agencies accepted consulting contracts from the corporations they are rating. Recent controversies in the mainstream stock brokerage, investment banking, and accounting worlds have shown the potential for conflicts of interest when a firm accepts consulting fees from a company that it evaluates or monitors.

In general, the funding prospects for rating organizations are better than those for infomediary researchers because financial services companies are increasingly willing to pay well for the product they provide. Although it is unclear just how large a market the financial community will support, it will, in all probability, be substantial.

The financial markets can go far in supporting rating groups, but the question of how to ensure quality standards in their work remains. This is a task with which government might help. In one such effort, in early 2004 a coalition of fifteen European SRI rating services announced that they had received funding from the European Commission to develop a set of corporate sustainability and responsibility research-quality standards.[10] Government might also directly or indirectly ensure that the details and ratings compiled by these organizations find their way to other stakeholders outside the financial community. Addressing this last challenge is particularly important for broadening the debate.

Demystifying and Debating the Data

With the support of the financial markets and government, infomediaries and rating agencies are likely to bring valuable data on corporations' ability to generate long-term wealth to the attention of investors, consumers, employees, communities, and the general public. But it is not clear what will happen if these stakeholders are not adequately informed or motivated enough to put these tools to use. Many still find the workings of finance and business a mystery. They give little thought to the implications of basic concepts such as price, returns, and the corporation's appropriate role in society.

Efforts to demystify finance and business, and to debate their roles, though substantial, will be worth undertaking. In order for investors, consumers, and other stakeholders to send messages to the corporate community about social and environmental initiatives, they must be well-informed and able to reflect on the true values of their society. For consumers to reward one company for a credible job in managing working conditions at its overseas suppliers and punish a second for not doing so, for example, they must understand the complexities of operating overseas and what are and are not reasonable goals for corporations to meet. The alternatives to informed debate are uninformed protests and the occasional bad actor punished as an example for others; neither will lead to consistent recognition of the efforts that deserve reward and those that do not.

The business and financial communities are themselves in large part to blame for the ignorance and mistrust built into the current system. They have long spoken in obscure language that fosters an ill-informed public. Investors are confused by complicated financial products. Employees lack the financial skills they need to understand the businesses for which they work. Consumers understand little about how the products and services they purchase are produced, or by whom. It is not surprising that an atmosphere of mistrust prevails.

Demystification

In the SRI and CSR worlds, community development financial institutions, employee-owned corporations, and transparent large businesses have shown what demystification and education look like in practice. Yet what they have done to educate borrowers, employees, and consumers is but a fraction of what the mainstream could accomplish if it chose to empower its stakeholders.

Community Development Financial Institutions

Community development financial institutions (CDFIs) are local banks, low-income credit unions, and community development loan funds that often assume a commitment to educate their customers and demystify the financial and business worlds. Two examples will illustrate this point: ShoreBank of Chicago, and Self-Help Credit Union of Durham, North Carolina.

Chicago's ShoreBank was among the first community development banks and has become an international model for community banking since its founding in 1973. In 2004, it served twenty-two predominately low-income, African-American neighborhoods in Chicago, Detroit, and Cleveland, and had assets of $1.4 billion. It has worked through a network of for-profit and nonprofit subsidiaries to revitalize these neighborhoods.

Education about finance and business is part of ShoreBank's development tactics. The bank is one of the principal lenders to faith-based groups in Chicago, with more than eight hundred African-American churches among its customers. ShoreBank works closely with these churches, as well as the other nonprofit organizations, to improve their financial management and banking skills. In meetings with its borrowers, the bank usually helps them gain access to appropriate resources for business and financial management. Through its nonprofit subsidiary, ShoreBank Neighborhood Institute, it trains low-income residents to save regularly under the nationwide Individual Development Accounts (IDA) program that matches new savings. Its Wealth Creation Initiatives program conducts seminars to help clients grow their money by explaining the basics of financial services, teaching wealth-creation strategies, and developing new behavior patterns.

Self-Help Credit Union takes a similar approach, but serves a rural clientele. Self-Help is one of the larger and better-established members of a network of community development credit unions that has grown up recently around the United States. Many of its financial services are targeted to women and minorities. Educating both its lenders and the public about financial matters is part of its daily work. It has, for example, focused on educating the general public and policymakers about the abuses of predatory lending to the poor. It founded the Center for Responsible Lending in North Carolina, which has issued research studies on the extent of this problem nationwide and helped North Carolina and other states pass legislation to control it.

Self-Help is also a strong supporter of charter schools that provide free education in low-income neighborhoods, and makes lending for their creation one of its priorities.

In addition, this credit union seeks to strengthen the business skills of the social service providers to whom it targets much of its lending. It is the largest lender to child care providers in North Carolina, where it has supported the creation of facilities that can accommodate over twenty thousand children since its founding in 1980. It has prepared a manual for these providers called *The Business Side of Child Care*, and publishes a similar guide for its borrowers in the business of supportive housing, which includes shelters for the disabled, those with AIDS, and others needing special assistance.

Employee-Owned Companies

Commitments to education are also implicit in the structure of employee-owned companies, where workers need to know how businesses are run and difficult decisions are made. The Antioch Company, headquartered in Yellow Springs, Ohio, is an example of a company where employee education and empowerment are part of the corporate culture. Employees own 100 percent of this producer and marketer of scrapbooks and photo albums that had $400 million in revenues in 2003. Under the leadership of the Morgan family since its founding in 1926, the company established profit sharing in 1929 and reaffirmed its commitment to employee involvement in 1979 when it established an employee stock ownership plan (ESOP). Each year, the company contributes to the ESOP account of its domestic employees a combination of stock and cash based on compensation (approximately 21 percent of compensation in 2004). Employees who have been with the firm for eighteen to twenty years today have ESOP accounts worth over $1 million. In addition, a cash profit sharing plan sets aside between 3 percent and 5 percent of profits to be distributed semiannually in equal payments to all employees worldwide; the payout in the first half of 2004 was approximately $1,300 per employee.

The Antioch Company has taken several steps to ensure that employees understand its business and financials. In one unusual initiative, employees have the right to elect two members to its nine-member board of directors and select another three to attend and participate fully in all meetings, but without voting privileges. The goal is for all locations with a hundred or more employees to have a representative on the board. Board meetings are open to all employees, and are occasionally held in auditoriums to accommodate substantial numbers of employees. In addition, the company's chief executive, Lee Morgan, visits its major domestic facilities each quarter (and international facilities annually) to share with employees not only the finances of all divisions but the decisions of the board on everything from business strategy to CEO evaluations.

Yellow Springs is home to a second employee-owned firm, YSI Incorporated, whose founders drew their social commitment from educators at Antioch College. The company was founded in 1948 and since 1983 has been 100 percent owned by its U.S. employees, who numbered approximately three hundred in 2002. This manufacturer of scientific instruments used for environmental and water monitoring (with $60 million in 2003 revenues) also involves employees in the environmental management of the firm, is an endorser of the CERES environmental principles, and publishes a detailed sustainability report documenting its social and environmental policies and practices.[11]

Transparent Large Businesses

For companies in the mainstream business community that are committed to CSR, the question of how much they should educate their investors, customers, and other stakeholders on the challenges they face is increasingly important. The approach recently taken by Gap Inc. illustrates how CSR reporting can serve to educate.

When this clothing retailer released its first corporate social responsibility report in 2004, it took a detailed look at the difficulties of managing networks of overseas suppliers. Its willingness to open itself to criticism in the interest of disclosure was exemplified when it included in the report its internal auditors' findings on working conditions at the approximately three thousand facilities approved for use in 2003. Although it found few violations of child labor or forced labor standards, it did report that between 10 percent and 25 percent of the factories in six of the eleven regions from which it sourced products had violations relating to payment of the local minimum wage.

In its 2004 report the company also unveiled a preliminary version of a factory rating system that it is developing, showing aggregate ratings of 324 facilities in six countries. The report also included four case studies of difficult standards compliance issues that had arisen in Guatemala, Lesotho, Cambodia, and China. These case studies dramatize the complex factors involved in attempting to implement fair labor standards internationally. In examining these current difficulties, Gap's report also demonstrated how multistakeholder partnerships can help build credibility and trust. The report itself was the result of one such partnership; the firm had conducted a two-year dialogue with a group of socially responsible investors including the As You Sow Foundation, the Calvert Group, the Center for Reflection, Education and Action, Domini Social Investments, and the Interfaith Center on Corporate Responsibility.

The Situation Today

Few mainstream financial institutions make the kind of commitment to basic education and demystification that CDFIs make. Few businesses are willing to empower employees in decision making through a thorough understanding of financials. Few major corporations are willing to expose themselves to criticism by educating their customers on the difficult business decisions they face every day. Nevertheless, if investors, employees, and customers are to assess the long-term wealth-creating abilities of the business world, then more of this demystification and education will need to take place.

Debate About Fundamentals

The demystification and education process can address the obscurity of specific business language and practices. However, three fundamental questions about the concepts on which today's business world is based need also to be addressed. What is the meaning of return on investment? What are the implications of price? What is the role of corporations as citizens? If long-term wealth generation is to become a guiding principle throughout society, then understanding of these concepts will need to become more sophisticated and better integrated into the daily decisions of consumers and investors.

A look at current debates about the meaning of these three fundamentals will help illustrate both the achievements of today's pioneering work in the SRI, CSR, and social entrepreneurship worlds, and the distance we still need to cover to bring these discussions into the mainstream.

Return on Investment

The emerging fields of social venture capital and venture capital philanthropy approach the question of returns from different directions, but they still ask the same question: What is the meaning of a "social return" and how can it be measured?

Investors' Circle is a network of venture capitalists who invest in companies that provide commercial solutions to social and environmental problems. Over the years, its members have invested in companies such as Earth's Best, the producer of organic baby foods, and Energia Global, a manufacturer of renewable power, cogeneration, and energy efficiency products in Latin America. Woody Tasch, who heads Investors' Circle, describes the group as seeking an ERR (an external rate of return) that captures social and environmental impacts, as well as an IRR (an internal rate of return) that measures traditional financial rewards. "To IRR is human, to ERR is divine," asserts Tasch, highlighting the difference between the ERR concept and the values of the traditional venture capitalist.[12]

In the philanthropic world, Jed Emerson is among those pioneering work on the concept and calculation of social returns. While working at the Roberts Enterprise Development Fund (now known as REDF), he promoted the concepts of a "social venture capital approach to philanthropy" and support for "social purpose business ventures." Known as the Homeless Economic Development Fund in an earlier incarnation, as of 2004 REDF supported a portfolio of twenty businesses that provide employment opportunities for approximately six hundred homeless and very low-income individuals. It measures and reports on what it calls the "social return on investments (SROI)" for each of these businesses. Some of the components of SROI are relatively quantifiable, such as community tax savings, decreased social service costs, and individuals' increased income, but it also seeks to capture less tangible elements, such as self-esteem.[13]

Emerson has gone on to develop the concept of *blended value returns*, which seek to value both social and financial returns on investments, blurring the line between corporate social responsibility, social enterprise, social investing, strategic philanthropy, and sustainable development.[14] In July 2004, along with Timothy Freundlich and Shari Berenbach of the Calvert Social Investment Foundation, he published a white paper proposing a "unified investment strategy" that would allow investors to achieve "financial, social, and environmental goals."[15]

The Implications of Price

Tod Murphy opened the Farmers Diner in Barre, Vermont, in 2002 with one simple goal: to get 60 to 80 percent of the food he served in the diner from producers located within seventy miles. So that customers won't forget the source of the food the diner offers and the value of a local economy, the placemats on the tables remind them that the meat on their plates traveled only the distance from a small processing plant down the road, rather than the fifteen hundred miles that food travels on average to reach a restaurant table. To gain access to locally raised meats, Murphy found that he needed to start a USDA-licensed meat-processing plant himself—Vermont Smoke & Cure. To serve locally grown, organic vegetables, he found he needed to cultivate relations with a network of local growers. This creation—or re-creation—of a local infrastructure is part of the diner's story. The story is an appealing one, and Murphy plans to capitalize on its appeal when he expands his current single operation to multiple restaurants in Vermont and other regions.

The story of the Farmers Diner gets woven into the price of the items on the menu. As Bill McKibben pointed out in an article on local economies in *Harper's* magazine, this diner is an "example of embracing a certain kind of inefficiency," an inefficiency that means building a processing plant in order to tell a story about locally produced goods, even if the items on the menu don't end up costing less than those at McDonald's.[16] The prices on the menu are certainly reasonable, but they can't beat the fast food chains. One story that drives consumers in the marketplace is that of efficiency: the producer who gets the highest-quality goods to the market at the lowest price wins. Another story is that of status: some will pay for the prestige that a $10,000 watch brings, although it tells time no better than a $10 timepiece. The Farmers' Diner raises another question: Are consumers willing to pay for the story of environmental and local value?[17]

The Role of Corporation as Citizen

The term *corporate citizenship* is a fundamental one in the CSR vocabulary, usually encompassing companies' responsibility to the full range of their shareholders. Professor Sandra Waddock of Boston College's Carroll School of Management offers the following definition:

> Good corporate citizens . . . treat well the entire range of stakeholders who risk capital in, have an interest in, or are linked to the firm through primary or secondary impacts by developing respectful, mutually beneficial operating practices and by working to maximize sustainability of the natural environment.[18]

Working in conjunction with Sandra Waddock and her colleague Samuel Graves, *Business Ethics* magazine, under the editorship of Marjorie Kelly, has published a list of its "100 Best Corporate Citizens" each year since 2000. The *Business Ethics* list scores companies across seven stakeholder categories: share owners, community, minorities and women, employees, environment, non-U.S. stakeholders, and customers. The companies that made the top ten in 2004 were Fannie Mae, Procter & Gamble, Intel, St. Paul Travelers, Green Mountain Coffee Roasters, Deere & Company, Avon Products, Hewlett-Packard, Agilent Technologies, and Ecolab.[19]

There are those who balk at the term corporate citizenship because they worry that it implies that corporations should benefit from the Bill of Rights and other Constitutional protections that are possessed by natural persons. Among such skeptics are those at the Community Environmental Legal Defense Fund (CELDF). Located in rural Pennsylvania, CELDF initially worked with local communities to pass laws banning corporate ownership of farms and the spreading of processed, but potentially toxic, municipal sludge on farmland. When its success at passing such local ordinances was overturned in part as a result of corporate lobbying at the state level, CELDF launched a legal and legislative campaign to stop the state from preempting the ability of local governments to adopt ordinances. Porter and Licking Townships in Clarion County then became the first municipal governments to

adopt binding ordinances refusing to recognize corporate constitutional rights.[20] In a similar vein, in California, the Berkeley City Council passed an advisory resolution in June 2004 in support of amending
the U.S. Constitution to specify that corporations do not have the same
rights as persons. Previously, Point Arena, California, had become the
first city in the United States to pass such a resolution.

Also embedded in the concepts of SRI and CSR is the flip side of
the citizenship question: Do individuals in their roles as investors, consumers, employees, and community members have "citizen-like" obligations to the corporations they encounter every day? Investors can vote
on matters of common concern and choose their representatives on the
board of directors. Consumers can support the creation of a certain
kind of society through their purchases. Employees can affiliate themselves with an employer or a union that represents certain social ideals.
Viewed through this lens, the "responsible" in socially responsible
investing refers as much to the investors as to the corporations in which
they invest.

✎✎✎

The previous chapter discussed comprehensive disclosure of
data on corporations' social and environmental records, and this chapter highlighted the importance of analysis and debate based on that
data. In the next chapter, we will turn our attention to the final link in
the chain: the actual market mechanisms that will steer corporations to
the public interest.

CHAPTER SIX

The Last Step:
Consequences in the Marketplace

CONSEQUENCES IN THE MARKETPLACE WILL BE OF CRUCIAL importance in steering corporations toward the public interest; without these consequences, disclosure of data, analysis, and debate will fail to realize their full potential to influence. Stakeholders as they interact with corporations, investors as they evaluate a company's prospects, and consumers as they make their daily decisions, all have the opportunity to create consequences. They are Adam Smith's invisible hand, which guides the businessperson, who "neither intends to promote the public interest, nor knows how much he is promoting it," to act in ways that benefit society. We will see in this chapter that these consequences can occur through three mechanisms that have been explored in recent years by the socially responsible investment and corporate social responsibility communities: targeted engagement, reallocation of assets, and broad public discourse on corporations and society.

Although some recent progress has been made in the development of these three mechanisms, we have only tantalizing glimpses of the meaningful actions that could be taken because the markets as they currently stand still don't send corporate managers strong enough messages when it comes to questions of long-term wealth and the public interest. With government's help, each of these mechanisms can be strengthened and expanded to transform today's marketplace into one that can act more meaningfully in these areas.

Targeted Engagement

The term *targeted engagement* refers here to a range of dialogues between stockowners and corporate managers on nonfinancial matters. One of the goals of targeted engagement is to change the vocabulary business managers use in discussing their relationships and responsibilities to society and the environment. This shift in vocabulary is a crucial first step in communicating to managers the new and changing expectations of stakeholders and in aligning corporate actions with the public interest. Without engagement in dialogue on targeted social and environmental issues, a shift in corporate behavior in these areas is unlikely to occur. As owners of publicly traded corporations, investors are uniquely qualified to engage in dialogue with corporate management. For this reason, investors engaging managers on social and environmental issues have already done much to shift the vocabulary that frames corporations' relationships to society and are likely to prompt further shifts in the future.

Investors today are increasingly willing to engage management on nonfinancial issues. This is a departure from the once widely accepted principle in the investment community, the *Wall Street Walk*, which held that if investors didn't like what management was doing, they should sell their shares and walk away. Today, institutional investors with billions of dollars in assets cannot simply walk away from their holdings because their portfolios are so large and diversified that they encompass all major asset classes. In effect, they "own the economy." Consequently, it is argued by advocates of "fiduciary capitalism," such as Professors James Hawley and Andrew Williams, that these investors' concern should not be the performance of an individual company in their portfolio but rather of the economy as a whole, of which their holdings are simply a reflection. Their fiduciary obligation is not to make sure that they are invested in a particular stock or bond that fares well, but rather that they are invested generally in an economy that is thriving.[1]

As a consequence, over the past decade mainstream institutional investors have become increasingly willing to engage management on the financial implications of corporate governance issues, such as the independence of boards of directors and conflicts of interest among auditors. Although these investors' concerns are primarily financial, the line between corporate governance issues and social and environmental issues has begun to blur. Corporate governance issues, including CEO compensation, are of concern to those in SRI while the financial implications of social and environmental matters, including climate change, are increasingly important to corporate managers, boards of directors, and mainstream institutional investors.

Four examples of the effective use of targeted engagement illustrate how it can shift business considerations toward the long term: investor use of shareholder proxy resolutions, particularly in the United States; engagement by major financial services firms with corporate management on CSR issues, particularly in the United Kingdom; the activity of national and international coalitions of institutional investors formed to address CSR issues in specific industries; and relationship investing, when investors take ownership positions in companies with poor corporate governance in order to improve their performance.

Shareholder Proxy Resolutions

Investors in a publicly traded corporation receive a proxy statement prior to its annual meeting, providing details on important matters of business on which they are entitled to vote. U.S. securities laws and regulations have historically ensured that investors can, with relative ease, place resolutions on the proxy statement. These resolutions provide investors with an effective means to communicate with one another and with management on issues they believe are of importance. Since the early 1970s, church investors—and others in the SRI world—have filed numerous resolutions on social and environmental issues.

Coordinating their work primarily through the Interfaith Center on Corporate Responsibility, originally under the leadership of Timothy Smith and subsequently Sister Patricia Wolf, these investors now file hundreds of resolutions each year on issues such as overseas labor contracting, environmental stewardship, nondiscrimination, militarism, marketing practices in developing countries, and CEO compensation.[2]

When they are presented for a vote at the annual meeting, or when management negotiates with the filers prior to the meeting, these resolutions create a dialogue between the investors and management. In this way, social and environmental concerns are shared with management and with other stockowners. Some assert that shareholder resolutions lack real clout because those opposed by management rarely receive a majority vote, and those few that do are strictly advisory and can be ignored by the company. However, the explicit or implicit threat of the filing of a shareholder resolution can be a powerful motivation for corporate management to engage in serious dialogue with stockowners. In fact, many dialogues with management result in successful negotiations without resolutions having to be filed. During thirty-five years of dialogue and filings, this process has done much to introduce social and environmental issues and vocabulary to the business community and has prompted meaningful change.

In one recent example, dialogue between concerned investors and Procter & Gamble (P&G) resulted in this consumer products giant launching a line of fair trade–certified coffees without the filing of a resolution. Socially concerned shareholders, including Domini Social Investments and the faith-based Center for Reflection, Education and Action, entered into a dialogue with the company during a period when activist nonprofits such as Oxfam had targeted the company and other coffee roasters in a global consumer campaign. These groups called P&G's attention to the crisis created by the steep drop in the price of coffee, threatening the ability of the governments of coffee-dependent economies, such as those of Ethiopia and Uganda, to provide basic social services to their people, while also threatening the livelihoods of small coffee growers in Latin America and elsewhere. This action was only part of a growing movement in support of fair trade coffee—coffee for which a guaranteed "fair" price is paid that supports democratically run and worker-owned coffee farms and their often ecologically beneficial agricultural practices.

After extensive dialogue with these stockowners and activist organizations, P&G agreed to launch a new line of fair trade–certified coffees under its Millstone label in 2003. P&G is one of the largest coffee roasters in the world and the largest seller of coffee in the United States. The company is now in a position to become a leading seller of fair trade–certified coffee in this country.[3]

Engagement by Major Financial Services Firms

In the United Kingdom, investors concerned with CSR have made engagement with management a primary focus. Many of that country's largest financial services companies now assert that it is appropriate to engage the management of the companies in which they invest on a range of social and environmental issues on behalf of their investors. Such British firms as Aviva plc (Morley Fund Management), ISIS Asset Management, HBOS plc (Insight Investment), and Henderson Global Investors have in-house SRI teams, sometimes known as "green teams," that research the social and environmental records of the companies in which they invest. When these internal advocates encounter issues of concern in areas such as human rights or the environment, they engage corporate management in dialogue, advocate change, and then communicate progress—or lack of it—to their investor clients. These green teams are empowered to speak on behalf of the total assets of their firms, which can be in the tens or hundreds of billions of dollars. Their communications consequently carry great weight.

ISIS Asset Management was a pioneer in this engagement process. The firm's commitment to social and environmental issues extends back to the Friends Provident insurance company, which was founded in the early nineteenth century to provide insurance for Quakers. Through a complicated series of mergers in recent years, Friends Provident has become incorporated into ISIS, where it continues to exercise its influence. Throughout its history, Friends Provident screened out the stocks of companies involved in alcohol, tobacco, armaments, and gambling. In the early 1980s, it became a leader in the SRI movement in the U.K. with the launch of its Stewardship Funds, which combined these screens with others covering the environment, human rights, and additional issues. In the early 2000s, then operating as ISIS Asset Management, it created a research and engagement practice called "responsible engagement overlay," otherwise known as "reo®," which it now applies to all its equity assets. A team headed by Karina Litvack publishes a quarterly "reo® report" for the company's investor clients. The 2004 first-quarter report highlighted ways in which the firm had engaged with companies on environmental management and climate change (38 engagements), biodiversity (23), labor standards (19), human rights (13), transparency (42), bribery and corruption (165), and corporate governance (61). ISIS also manages the Stewardship Funds, which are screened on social and environmental criteria and had assets under management of approximately $2.7 billion (£1.5 billion) as of 2004. In October 2004, ISIS completed its planned merger with F&C Asset Management, at which time it assumed the F&C name. This merger will substantially increase assets under management and hence the firm's potential to influence corporations through its engagement.

Among the foremost advocates of the engagement strategy in the U.K. is Craig Mackenzie, who heads up the "investor responsibility" team at Insight Investment, a subsidiary of HBOS. Under Mackenzie's direction, Insight engages with companies held in HBOS's almost $125 billion (£69 billion) investments on a variety of social and environmental issues and offers similar services to other institutional investors. It does so both because it believes that investment returns can benefit from such engagement and because it believes that investors have a moral responsibility toward companies in which they invest. It places particular emphasis on global norms and principles as a guide to its engagement. In spring 2004, it reported in its regularly published *Investor Responsibility Bulletin* that it had engaged with 114 companies in the first quarter of that year on issues including responsible supply chain management (forty-nine engagements), biodiversity (twenty-one engagements), board remuneration (twenty-six), and the One Million Sustainable Homes project (thirteen). Insight also manages two socially screened funds, the European Ethical Fund and the Evergreen Fund.

Coalition Activities

To act effectively and efficiently, SRI investors form coalitions to address industry-wide issues and to promote change. Three examples show how these efforts result in broad dialogue.

- *The Carbon Disclosure Project (CDP)* was launched in 2000 to encourage the world's five hundred largest companies to disclose the level of their greenhouse gas emissions. CDP's November 2003 request for data was signed by some ninety-five institutional investors with combined assets of $10 trillion.[4]
- *The Extractive Industries Transparency Initiative (EITI)*, launched at the World Summit on Sustainable Development in September 2002 by the British government working in partnership with various companies and nonprofit organizations, including Publish What You Pay, seeks to increase disclosure by multinational corporations in the natural resource extraction business of royalties and other payments they make to local governments. EITI

argues that these payments are often associated with government corruption or human rights scandals and has assembled a coalition of thirty-five institutional investors with $3 trillion under management to endorse this call for action.[5]

- *The Investor Network on Climate Risk (INCR)* in the United States, led by CERES, includes eight state treasurers, four labor pension fund leaders, the comptroller of New York City, and one foundation president. The INCR focuses on the financial risks posed by climate change. In April 2004, a number of INCR members called on the Securities and Exchange Commission to mandate corporate disclosure of such risks.[6]

Relationship Investing

Relationship investing is a technique pioneered during the 1990s by Robert A.G. Monks and Ralph Whitworth, among others. Relationship investors acquire substantial stock holdings in poorly performing firms explicitly to seek improvements in their corporate governance. In a sense the opposite of "best in class" investing, this approach is based on the theory that turning around poor corporate management practices holds the promise of delivering superior stock performance.

In their 2002 publication *Capitalism Without Owners Will Fail,* Robert Monks and Allen Sykes see what they call specialist investing and relationship investing as a future trend. *Specialist investors* would consist of individual funds specializing in large holdings (for example, 4 to 5 percent of a company's shares) in a limited number (some eight to ten) of companies. *Relationship investors* would consist of a number of funds with similar holdings that would coordinate their communications with corporate managers on a select number of issues. Both types of funds would scrutinize all aspects of the companies' businesses and communicate closely with management.[7] To date, only investors primarily concerned with corporate governance (that is, issues related to stockowners) have taken a relationship investing approach, but nothing prevents a similar tactic from being used by those concerned with social and environmental issues.

Targeted Engagement to Date

To date, targeted engagements have been effective to a limited extent and on specific issues with specific companies. They have required considerable efforts to achieve relatively modest goals. Management can, and still often does, simply ignore them. To increase the effectiveness of this kind of action—and the systematic changes in the corporate managers' attention to these issues that would follow—the position of stakeholders, including stockowners, needs to be strengthened.

One way to achieve this is through an increased professionalization of corporate boards of directors, who ultimately have the power to hire and fire management. In the wake of the financial and accounting scandals of the early 2000s, U.S. lawmakers and regulators have sought to make corporate boards and auditors more independent from management and less prone to conflicts of interest through passage of the Sarbanes-Oxley Act and strengthened listing requirements for stock exchanges. These regulations are intended to strengthen the hand of the board of directors in preventing management abuses and to ensure that stockowners' interests are adequately represented.

Another proposal made in 2003 by the U.S. Securities and Exchange Commission (SEC) may make boards more responsive to stockowners by improving stockowners' access to the board nomination process. In response to a rule-making petition filed by several unions including the AFL-CIO and American Federation of State, County and Municipal Employees, the SEC has proposed increasing stockowners' ability to include their own nominees for boards of directors on the proxy statements that corporations send to shareholders.

Still under consideration as of mid-2004, this proposal would give large stockowners the ability to place their nominees for the board on a company's proxy statement if 35 percent of stockowners withheld support for a nominee to the board, or if a majority supported a proposal from a stockowner with a 1 percent holding in the company to have its nominee included on the proxy.[8] If adopted, this proposal would mean that when boards of directors are unresponsive, stockowners would have increased power to oppose and replace them. In addition, an increasing number of investors are currently voting against boards of directors who fail to see to it that management implements resolutions receiving a majority vote.

The Community Reinvestment Act in the United States might provide another model for empowering stakeholders in their dialogue with management. This law allows community groups to petition federal regulators to block bank mergers or acquisitions if they believe that the banks in question have an unsatisfactory record on community lending. The threat of future intervention by community groups at this single, but critical, point in business decision making has done much to focus the attention of bank managers on their community lending records and extracted substantial commitments to such lending. Finding analogous mechanisms for other stakeholders and other industries is an option worth exploring.

Asset Reallocation

Reallocation of assets refers here to the redirection of investments or purchases from many of today's mainstream entities to those that do a better job of taking long-term wealth creation into account. The ability to attract investors and consumers is a classic market indicator, and the business community pays unfailing attention to it. For this reason, reallocation of assets can work powerfully to redirect its attention.

Four asset reallocation initiatives in the investment community are microlending, community investing, social venture capital funds, and screened funds. Preferential purchasing among consumers, based on social and environmental considerations, also holds promise as a tool for directing corporations to the public interest.

Microlending and Community Investing

The recent growth in microlending illustrates how reallocation of assets to microfinance institutions working with the most needy sectors of society can create long-term wealth. Built on the concept that the economically disadvantaged, who often have no access to traditional banks, are in fact good credit risks, microlending has cultivated economic self-sufficiency among the poor and strengthened communities throughout the developing world.

Muhammad Yunus of the Grameen Bank in Bangladesh is one of the pioneers of this kind of lending. In the late 1970s and early 1980s, Grameen Bank began making small unsecured loans to women, primarily, in rural villages, so they could start small businesses. The program, which has grown dramatically since then, works as follows. Each borrower must join a support group that meets regularly to share challenges and successes. The groups assure repayment of the loans (almost 99 percent are repaid), while also empowering their women members to change their lives. In Bangladesh, for example, they are asked to adopt a set of guidelines called "Sixteen Decisions," which, among other things, urge them to make increased use of family planning and turn away from the traditional system of dowries in marriages.[9] Through late 2004, the bank had disbursed approximately $4.6 billion in such loans. In 2003, Grameen expanded its lending in Bangladesh to an unlikely clientele: beggars. The bank makes small interest-free loans to these people, who wear badges identifying themselves as Grameen Bank members and use the loans to begin income-generating activities, such as selling popular consumer products door to door or at the place of begging. The bank expects approximately twenty-five thousand beggars to join this program in 2004.[10]

The microlending paradigm has inspired a proliferating network of microcredit financial services institutions around the world.

- *Accion International,* which began microlending in Latin America in the 1970s, was among the earliest. Through 2003, it had made some $5.8 billion in loans to 3.2 million clients, 97 percent of which had been repaid. In 2003 alone, it disbursed $1.1 billion in loans with an average size of $554.[11]
- *Women's World Banking* promotes the economic development of women around the world through microfinancing. As of 2003, it worked with twenty-six women-led affiliated microlending organizations in twenty countries; these organizations had served over 580,000 clients with loans averaging $356 through the end of 2001.[12]

In the United States, community investing is similarly founded on the premise that today's mainstream financial institutions are doing a poor job of providing economically disadvantaged communities with the access to the capital that can improve their daily lives and create a richer, more viable society. A variety of community-oriented banks, credit unions, and loan funds have sprung up that are dedicated to serving these communities through affordable housing financing, small business lending, and financial education programs. According to the Social Investment Forum, as of 2003 community development banks in the United States had $7.2 billion in assets, community development credit unions $2.7 billion, and community development loan funds $3.6 billion.[13]

City National Bank in Newark, New Jersey, is one example of a community development bank. The only bank in the state that is owned and operated by African Americans, it has made a notable commitment to urban revitalization, particularly through support of the local church community. A different model with the same goal is the Quitman/ Tri-County Credit Union, located in the Mississippi Delta, one of the poorest regions in the country. Founded in 1981 to help those in the region who lacked access to local financial institutions, it has made over $20 million in loans to members for purchases of homes and cars, tuition payments, or consolidation of bills. Another variation on this same theme is the Institute for Community Economics, one of the oldest community development loan funds in the United States. Its specialty is lending to cooperative-owned community land trusts, including owners of mobile homes wishing to acquire their mobile home parks.

Over the past few decades, efforts have been made to certify financial institutions that fill the community development role in order to support their activities. In 1994, the U.S. Treasury Department established the Community Development Financial Institutions (CDFI) Fund to promote their growth. It provides a certification process through which CDFIs can be formally acknowledged. In addition, its Bank Enterprise Awards Program channels additional dollars to CDFIs. In July 2004, it awarded $17 million to forty-nine banks and savings and loans serving economically distressed communities.[14] The fund also provides financial and technical assistance to qualifying organizations.

The U.S. Treasury Department has a certification program that awards a similar Community Development Credit Union (CDCU) status. The National Federation of Community Development Credit Unions (NFCDCU) is a trade association of over two hundred CDCU credit unions serving low-income neighborhoods with combined assets of more than $2 billion. In July 2004, NFCDCU launched a program to help its members fight payday lending in low-income neighborhoods.[15] Payday lending is a form of predatory lending prevalent in low-income communities; high-cost, short term loans are made to cash-strapped borrowers who pledge repayment from future payroll checks or social security payments. The association is also increasing its emphasis on training members to offer financial education programs to those they serve.

Social Venture Capital Funds

A growing network of social venture capital funds includes both environmental and social goals in their investment criteria, redirecting funds from traditional venture capital projects to those with a greater social and environmental impact. Among the groups coordinating such efforts in the United States is the Investors' Circle. Founded in 1992, its members had invested $90 million in 147 enterprises through 2004. Investors' Circle has helped launch Commons Capital, a $13.5 million venture capital fund seeking both financial returns and a positive social and environmental story. Under the leadership of William Osborn, Commons Capital invests in companies that promote clean energy, the environment, education, and health care. Among its initial investments were CellTech Power, a fuel cell company; H2Gen, a generator of hydrogen from natural gas; Niman Ranch, a natural foods meat company; and Sun & Earth, a natural household cleaning products firm.[16]

The Community Development Venture Capital Alliance (CDVCA) seeks to channel funds to low-income communities. This network of over one hundred venture capital funding organizations was formed in 1993. It uses venture capital to create jobs and businesses for low-income people in distressed communities. One of its members is Pacific Community Ventures, founded in 1999, which focuses on the San Francisco Bay Area. It raised $6.25 million for its first investment fund, and sought to raise $25 million for its second. Among its investments are First Light Destinations, a lodging company that hires at-risk youth, and Moving Solutions, an office and industrial location firm that employs low- and moderate-income residents of the city of San Jose.

Similarly, Boston Community Capital, originally a community development loan fund, now combines its affordable housing and small business lending with a venture capital arm that invests in "companies that are unlikely candidates for traditional exit vehicles"—that is, that may not grow to a size where they could become publicly traded. To date these have included a small family-owned machine shop, a minority-owned ethnic foods business, and a job placement service for welfare recipients and low-income workers.[17]

In Europe a number of "ecobanks" have sprung up, funding environmentally friendly businesses as part of their mission. Triodos Bank is one such entity, with operations in the Netherlands and England that specialize in lending to environmental and community development projects, including organic farming, wind power, and fair trade initiatives.

Social venture capital firms frequently speak of their simultaneous social and financial returns, and confront the question of whether incorporating social goals affects financial returns. Some funds, such as Commons Capital, strive for "traditional" venture returns, whereas others believe that sustainability goals imply slower growth and more modest returns. Commons Capital looks for companies that create a "sustainable economy" by, among other things, providing women and minorities access to capital, encouraging regular social and environmental audits and accountability to all stakeholders, and promoting consumer awareness of social and environmental issues. Pacific Community Ventures measures its social return in part by jobs created in low-income communities. More broadly, the movement is attempting to define itself more clearly. For example, Investors' Circle has joined with the Research Initiative on Social Entrepreneurship (RISE) at the Columbia Business School, and others, to map and define the social venture capital field.[18]

Screened Stock and Bond Funds

SRI investors who use social and environmental criteria in their decisions on which stocks or bonds to purchase are also reallocating assets. Negative screens, such as those precluding investments in tobacco, alcohol, gambling, and weapons companies, and positive screens, such as those favoring companies with strong records on the environment, employee relations, and diversity, have the effect of shifting investments toward companies that create long-term wealth. Screening has found particular success in the United States. According to figures compiled by the Social Investment Forum, as of 2003 $2.14 trillion were invested under at least one social screen, up from $529 billion in 1997. There were some two hundred socially screened, publicly traded mutual funds with combined assets of $151 billion. Many of these funds were subject to only a limited number of screens. For example, of the $151 billion, $124 billion had tobacco screens and $93.4 billion had alcohol screens but only $28.9 billion had environmental screens.[19]

What effect, if any, social and environmental screens funds have on investment performance or on companies' cost of capital is a subject of debate in the financial and business communities. Some SRI advocates argue that these screens help money managers avoid risks unrecognized by traditional stock analysts, help identify high-quality corporate management, and highlight companies that are attuned to emerging issues—all of which should certainly help boost performance.[20] But critics argue that, according to modern theories of portfolio management, any restriction on a universe of investments will increase its undiversified risk and reduce the appropriate level of financial return. Some assert that assets managed under such screens are insufficient to move stock prices. Others argue that social and environmental performance affects a company's overall reputation and that companies with stronger reputations can command higher price-to-earnings ratios in the stock markets and borrow at lower rates in the bond markets.[21]

Although the debate is still ongoing, considerable research indicates that, in general, social and environmental screening as recently practiced does not hurt a fund's financial performance. For example, a review of thirty-one socially screened mutual funds from 1990 to 1998 by Meir Statman, published in the *Financial Analysts Journal*, found that on average they outperformed their unscreened peers, but not by a statistically significant margin.[22] Similarly, an academic review of eighty studies on the links between CSR and financial performance published in 2001 noted that 58 percent of the studies found a positive relationship to performance, 24 percent found no relationship, 19 percent found a mixed relationship, and only 5 percent found a negative relationship.[23]

Preferential Purchasing

Corporations, governments, nonprofits, and individual consumers already practice what may be termed *preferential purchasing*. They may do this by opting to pay more for a product because of the company's social or environmental record, or they may show such a preference only when pricing is equal. They may opt to do business with a company only if it meets certain standards, or they may opt not to do any business at all with companies whose practices they believe are harmful. Whatever the particulars, the end result of preferential purchasing can be to channel dollars to companies that are creating, rather than destroying, long-term wealth.

Corporate management itself increasingly uses preferential purchasing for its own purposes. The drive for quality in manufacturing, which began in Japan in the 1970s and subsequently swept through the rest of the world, illustrates how powerful this tool can be. Many corporations now set strict quality standards for their vendors, often requiring ISO 9000 certification of quality standards before they will include a company among their suppliers. However, an increasing number of companies also require vendors to meet environmental standards. For example, Casio, the Japanese consumer products firm, publishes a "Green Procurement Standards Manual," surveys suppliers on the status of their environmental management systems, ranks them and their products on ecofriendliness, and gives preference to companies that qualify under its standards.[24] Similarly, in the United States many major corporations have programs dating back to the 1970s to increase contracts with minority- and women-owned suppliers. In 2003, General Motors spent some $7.2 billion on contracts with minority-owned businesses. Hewlett-Packard channeled approximately 21.9 percent of its total subcontracting for materials, goods, and services in the United States to women-owned and minority-owned companies.[25]

Governments can also use their purchasing power to promote environmental sustainability. In 1998, the Clinton administration initiated an Environmentally Preferential Purchasing Program that instructed agencies to "prevent waste and pollution by considering environmental impacts along with price and performance and other traditional factors when deciding what to buy."[26] Other national governments, including those of Canada, Germany, Norway, Switzerland, Denmark, and Japan, have adopted similar programs. In Japan, eighteen hundred businesses and 350 government organizations formed a "Green Procurement Network" to aid in implementing that country's policies.[27] The Republic of China in Taiwan issued a government procurement law in 1998 that requires government agencies to give preference to environmentally friendly products.[28] The Global Ecolabeling Network is an international coalition of twenty-six organizations, including several government-related agencies, that promotes and coordinates the development of "ecolabels" around the world.

Socially oriented nonprofits and consumers can also adopt this approach. Most notably today, there is a growing interest in organic and fair trade food products. The fair trade movement seeks to channel the purchasing power of consumers in developed countries toward support of artisans and farmers in developing countries, providing them with a fair price for their labor, encouraging them to own their own enterprises, and generally promoting an equitable international trade framework. By 2002, fair trade had become an international movement, with sales totaling $180 million in North America and $70.6 million in the Pacific Rim.[29] In 2001, European fair trade sales totaled almost €150 million.[30] Nonprofit organizations with a social mission take up this approach too. In late 2003, for example, Catholic Relief Services agreed to market fair trade coffee through nineteen thousand Catholic parishes throughout the United States.[31]

More generally, several U.S. organizations, such as the Center for a New American Dream and IdealsWork, are set up to help consumers incorporate social and environmental factors into their purchasing decisions.

Asset Reallocation to Date

Microlending and community investing, social venture capital funds, screened funds, and preferential purchasing are five examples of market mechanisms that can send positive signals to management about long-term wealth creation. Although these activities have gained momentum in recent years, they have yet to become an important part of the mainstream marketplace. Two steps in particular would facilitate and encourage their use: ensuring that consumers and investors have relevant data at the point of purchase, and fostering greater public debate about the nature of price and returns.

In the United States today, labeling requirements ensure that consumers have basic data about the ingredients in the food they purchase, calorie and fat content, and other nutritional information. Labels also provide information about manufactured products' country of origin. Organic certification of food and fair trade certification of coffee and crafts make available further information. These labels allow consumers to understand more fully the implications of the price being asked and to make a purchase informed more fully by their preferences. The more such data at the point of purchase, the easier it will be for consumers to express their preferences through the marketplace.

The expansion of data on labels could be required by regulators, imposed through independent, quasi-regulatory organizations, or implemented through industry trade associations. Voluntary labeling is also a possible approach, although various assertions, such as health claims, are closely regulated.

Better data could be made available to retail investors as well. Individuals purchasing stock currently are given little information on the social and environmental records of the companies in which they invest. Disclosure by corporations themselves—whether voluntary or mandatory—is a step in this direction. However, when this kind of information starts being integrated into the numerous newsletters, magazines, and electronic media outlets that provide small investors with information and recommendations, then it will be more likely to influence the markets.

On a more general level, increasingly sophisticated thinking about price and returns should be encouraged, one that captures the concept of long-term wealth in a way that transforms today's marketplace, with its excessive emphasis on maximum short-term returns and everyday low prices. To increase this sophistication, we need not only more data at the point of purchase but a new way to think about and calculate its value. For example, if people understood that what community development and microlending do is essentially internalize certain societal costs that the mainstream does not want to assume, they might better appreciate the long-term wealth these practices create, and this might affect their banking decisions, whether the returns such investments offer are equal to or lower than those of mainstream instruments.

Much needs to happen, though, before these concepts become an accepted part of the financial and consumer markets. Academia and the press can, and should, play a vital role. Perhaps even more important, a network of think tanks and study centers, through which these ideas and their ramifications can be explored and upon whose work a solid societal understanding can be built, could jump-start systematic change. The Institute for Responsible Investment at the Boston College Center for Corporate Citizenship, the Center for Business and Government at Harvard's Kennedy School of Government, and the Center for the Study of Fiduciary Capitalism at St. Mary's College of California are examples of the kind of research centers that, although currently still relatively modest in size, might eventually make up such a network.

Public Discourse

Public discourse refers here to broad-based social debate on the most difficult issues arising at the interface between corporations and society, issues where the appropriate lines between government and the private sector have yet to be drawn, where price and efficiency are secondary to public policy, where a viable society that acts in the long-term interest of its members is at stake. The crucial point of such discourse is not necessarily to reform corporate practice, but rather to criticize and reconstitute society's structure and government's role in it at a given time. The South Africa divestment movement of the 1970s and 1980s that was part of a worldwide campaign to dismantle that country's apartheid legal system is an example of how this kind of public discourse can result in major change.

Two developments in the investment community have already begun to promote this kind of discourse. First, recent government regulations in the United States, the United Kingdom, and elsewhere now force mutual funds, money managers, and pension funds to state more explicitly their positions on corporate social and environmental matters. Second, the socially responsible investment community uses social and environmental screens in its investment decisions.

Proxy Voting Disclosure

In January 2003, the U.S. Securities and Exchange Commission (SEC) issued new rulings requiring mutual funds and money managers to publish written policy guidelines on how they plan to vote on issues appearing on corporate proxy statements and to report to investors on their actual votes. Because many shareholder resolutions appearing on proxy statements deal with social and environmental issues, this ruling effectively forces mutual funds and money managers to take public positions on these important matters.

Prior to this ruling, mutual funds voted with little accountability to their investors. The votes of the mainstream funds often went with corporate management rather than in support of shareholder resolutions on social and environmental issues. Then, in the 1990s, a number of SRI mutual funds began publishing written guidelines on how they intended to vote on these resolutions, along with a public record of their actual votes. In November 2001, Domini Social Investments petitioned the SEC, asking that all mutual funds be required to make their guidelines and votes available to investors. The AFL-CIO and the International Brotherhood of Teamsters filed similar rule-making petitions. The SEC's new ruling was prompted in part as a result of these petitions.

At first glance, the SEC's decision to implement these disclosure requirements might seem a minor development. Its implications, however, are considerable. With the publication of the proxy voting guidelines in mid-2003 and public disclosure of actual votes starting in August 2004, the mainstream financial community has been drawn into public discourse on issues crucial to the public interest. In a column in the *Financial Times*, corporate governance consultant Stephen Davis called this development "the biggest bang in corporate governance since the U.S. government first mandated pension fund voting in 1988" and has aptly described it as the "financial equivalent of nutrition labels."[32]

Even before the disclosure of votes was required, the publication of voting guidelines had forced Wall Street financial services firms to take public positions demonstrating varying degrees of concern on matters of public interest. Merrill Lynch, for example, was typical of many in the mainstream financial community in its stance toward shareholders who wish to bring social and environmental matters to the attention of corporate managers. Its proxy voting guidelines state:

> The [Proxy Voting] Committee generally believes that annual shareholder meetings are inappropriate forums for discussion of larger social issues, and opposes shareholder resolutions "micromanaging" corporate conduct or requesting release of information that would not help a shareholder evaluate an investment in the corporation as an economic matter. While the Committee is generally supportive of proposals to require corporate disclosure of matters that seem relevant and material to the economic interests of shareholders, the Committee is generally not supportive of proposals to require disclosure of corporate matters for other purposes.[33]

By contrast, the proxy voting guidelines for INVESCO, a multibillion-dollar money management firm that is part of AIM Investments, a financial services corporation, publicly recognize the validity of several basic social principles:

> INVESCO believes that a corporation, if it is in a solid financial position and can afford to do so, has an obligation to return certain largesse to the communities in which it operates. INVESCO believes that the primary mission of a company is to be profitable. However, where a company has proven that it is able to sustain a level of profitability and the market price of a company's shares reflect [sic] an appropriate economic value for such shares, INVESCO will generally vote FOR certain social responsibility initiatives. . . . INVESCO will generally vote FOR
> - International Labor Organization Principles
> - Resolutions seeking Basic Labor Protections and Equal Employment Opportunity
> - Expanding EEO/Social Responsibility Reporting[34]

All U.S. mutual funds began publishing their actual votes on social and environmental issues on August 31, 2004. CSR advocates, unions, and the press have begun to analyze these votes and publicize the positions that mutual fund managers are taking on social, environmental, and corporate governance issues and the degree to which their votes have supported or opposed corporate management.[35] These disclosures are already compelling mainstream mutual fund management firms to confront publicly corporate management's handling of crucial social and environmental matters. They will also provide retail investors with additional information on which to assess the quality of the management of these funds, complementing the financial information they already have.

This important development in promoting public discourse could well extend beyond the United States. As of July 2004, the Canadian Securities Administrators was seeking comments on a proposal to implement a similar requirement for mutual funds in that country.[36]

In addition, since July 2000 the United Kingdom's approximately ten thousand pension funds have been required to state to what degree, if any, they take social and environmental factors into consideration in their investment decision making. A July 2004 report prepared for the Local Authority Pension Fund Forum found that, of the pension funds of fifty-five local authorities surveyed, 64 percent had delegated to their external fund managers responsibilities for engaging with corporations on corporate governance issues.[37] The implication of this study is that U.K. pension fund administrators are increasingly aware of social, environmental, and corporate governance issues, although implementation of engagement programs on these issues is not yet systematic.

Socially Responsible Investment Fund Screening

Screening portfolios on social and environmental criteria has proven effective in promoting public discourse on issues of broad societal concern. This ability to promote public debate is one of the greatest virtues of SRI screens.

Screening is effective in promoting prominent public discourse for two reasons. First, it allows investors to express their concerns in no uncertain terms to corporate management by shunning particular stocks or bonds. Second, it gives added force to their ongoing engagement and dialogue. As economist Albert Hirschman has pointed out in his book *Exit, Voice, and Loyalty,* voice without exit lacks force.[38] Translated into investment world terms, this means that the threat of divestment can increase the seriousness with which corporate management is likely to take dialogue and engagement.

Two Approaches

There are two basic approaches to SRI screening: excluding companies associated with whole industries or issues, and divesting individual companies within an industry. Each approach raises different questions for public debate. The first focuses on governmental policies and practices, the latter on the behavior of specific corporations.

As noted earlier, exclusionary screens have been used since the SRI movement began, when churches refused to invest in the "sin stocks" of alcohol, gambling, and tobacco firms. Since the development of modern-day SRI organizations in the 1970s, screens have also been applied to businesses associated with nuclear power, nuclear weapons, firearms, and the apartheid regime in South Africa. The South Africa divestment movement of the 1970s and 1980s shows clearly how forceful such screens can be in promoting public discourse. Driven by a desire to see the apartheid legal system in South Africa dismantled (not simply to see corporate practices there improved), many institutional investors around the world imposed South Africa screens on their investments during those years. In the United States, church investors acting through the Interfaith Center on Corporate Responsibility played a leading role early on. Public pension funds, universities, and other institutions soon followed suit. This divestment movement and the decision of investors to join it were the topic of ongoing press coverage and contributed substantially to the pressure on the South African government to change. Today's widespread SRI screens on tobacco and nuclear weapons similarly help keep before the public eye society's still-unresolved questions of how to cope with these difficult issues.

More recently, in 2000 the California Public Employees Retirement System (Cal/PERS), as part of changes in its investment policies for emerging markets, adopted a seven-factor scoring system to identify appropriate emerging-market countries in which to invest. One of these seven factors was productive labor practices. The fund then hired Verité, a U.S.-based research and consulting organization specializing in overseas contractor research, to conduct research in this area. Verité evaluated the labor practices in twenty-seven countries as they concerned freedom of association and collective bargaining, forced labor, child labor, equality and discrimination, and working conditions. In Verité's 2003 report to Cal/PERS, companies with the poorest scores on labor included Malaysia, Indonesia, India, China, and Pakistan.[39] The Verité research was then combined with research on the six other factors to assign a total country score; labor practices accounted for 17 percent of the total score and the six other factors for the remaining 83 percent of the score. Countries with the poorest overall scores in 2003 included Indonesia, Russia, Egypt, and Pakistan. The Cal/PERS rankings have provoked public debate about the records of specific countries. The fund reports that overall scores have improved over the years. Among the most improved countries from 2002 to 2003 were Poland and the Philippines.[40]

Screening individual companies in an industry on social and environmental grounds highlights the records of single firms relative to their peers. Most SRI money managers going beyond a pure-engagement approach impose such screens. As already noted, many assert that these screens help them avoid companies with long-term risks that may be overlooked by the mainstream and identify companies with high-quality management. This practice frequently promotes debates about larger societal issues as well. An SRI money manager might, for example, exclude the giant retailer Wal-Mart but include its peer Target on the grounds that the former lags in its overseas labor standards, employment of women and minorities, and support for local communities. But it is difficult to make this screening decision without also raising public debate about the question of the effect on other stakeholders of Wal-Mart's relentless pursuit of delivering goods to customers at low prices. The Wal-Mart screening decision therefore ultimately raises some particularly complicated questions, and becomes part of a larger public discourse on these issues.

SRI Indexes

SRI indexes have received much publicity in discussions about SRI and CSR in part because they publicly specify their screening techniques. A look at three of the more prominent ones demonstrates how their different screening approaches contribute in different ways to public discourse.

- *The Dow Jones Sustainability Indexes* are maintained by the Switzerland-based SAM Group. Each year SAM asks the twenty-five hundred largest companies in the Dow Jones Global Indexes to participate in its sustainability assessment process and scores those that participate relative to their industry peers. For the DJSI World Index, it then selects the 10 percent that have the highest score in each industry. No industry is necessarily excluded, although DJSI clients can opt for customized indexes with industry exclusions. This methodology is based in part on SAM's belief that "companies embracing sustainability will generate more long-term shareholder value than those ignoring the risks and opportunities."[41] The index methodology therefore focuses public debate on the question of the relationship between relative social and environmental performance and shareholder value.

- *The FTSE4Good Index* global series, in contrast, includes all companies that meet certain corporate social responsibility criteria. The only industry-wide exclusions are tobacco, weapons and nuclear weapons, and nuclear power and uranium production. Its screening criteria address issues of human rights, stakeholders, and the environment. An absolute level of performance against each criterion determines whether a company will be included. Companies are screened by the British SRI research firm EIRIS, along with an international network of other research providers. In July 2001, the FTSE Group launched the

FTSE4Good Index series, which it licenses to financial services firms. (FTSE contributes licensing fees from the FTSE4Good Index to UNICEF.) It raised the environmental criteria in May 2002 and added human rights criteria in April 2003. It plans to introduce supply chain labor standards criteria in 2004. The goal of this index series is to identify companies that "meet globally recognized corporate responsibility standards" and help the "development of responsible business practice around the world." The net effect is to promote public debate on appropriate international criteria for corporate conduct.[42]

- *The Domini 400 Social Index (DSI)*, maintained by KLD Research & Analytics, has a screening process that fosters broader, more free-form discourse on issues of corporate social responsibility. Its exclusionary screens are extensive, raising a range of fundamental questions about how corporations and society handle these challenging issues. The index excludes companies involved in alcohol, gambling, tobacco, military contracting, and nuclear power, and had a screen on companies in South Africa until 1993. The index is maintained at four hundred companies at all times, and companies once on the DSI are only rarely dropped—primarily in cases of mergers and acquisitions, but also for financial or social reasons. This relatively stable core of holdings implies a commitment to dialogue with corporations when they stray into questionable territory and to public debate on the appropriateness of their remaining on the index. KLD also publishes through its *Socrates* database extensive profiles of all four hundred companies on the DSI, as well as of the Standard & Poor's 500 Index companies that are not included. Domini Social Investments also carries on its Web site summary profiles of all the DSI companies.

As these examples indicate, different SRI screening processes raise issues for public debate in different ways. The variety of these approaches may at first confuse those who expect SRI to provide a single answer to these complicated questions. But the variety is emblematic of the ability of SRI screening to participate flexibly in the public discourse and is actually one of its strengths.

Public Discourse to Date

As we have seen in this section, public discourse on the appropriate role of corporations in society can be promoted in a variety of ways. The investment community can be forced to confront a range of social and environmental issues through their proxy voting policies. Pension funds can be encouraged by regulation, or prompted by their concerns about investment returns and the public good, to grapple with the non-financial aspects of their specific investment policies. Screening on social and environmental issues can raise issues of major concern to the public's attention.

Although initiatives already under way are bringing about some real change, they are far from completing the job. The ever-shifting relationship between corporations, government, and society continually prompts difficult questions about when and how corporations can best create long-term wealth. If a society is to be able to trust that both corporations and governments are acting in its best interest, these questions must be publicly debated and publicly resolved.

General discourse on these broad topics, however, is less easily defined and promoted than targeted engagement or reallocation of assets. For that reason, conceiving of and implementing the mechanisms to bring it about is a more challenging task. Certain regulatory requirements, such as forcing money managers to disclose their proxy votes, can bring about substantial change with relatively little effort.

What precisely the best mechanisms are for amplifying this type of discourse more broadly and systematically is not entirely clear.

At least four general principles for moving forward are likely to play an important role. First, the mainstream investment community, as unwilling as it may be to confront nonfinancial issues in its daily practice, can no longer stand on the sidelines in these debates. The social and environmental questions involved are too important and affect their long-term investments too directly for them to continue to avoid public participation. Similarly, pension funds need to more fully understand and embrace their roles as fiduciaries with long-term horizons, and for those in the public sectors, as organizations with a mission that encompasses the public good. Third, screening of portfolios on social and environmental grounds should be encouraged. It plays a valuable role in amplifying the voice of engagement and raises important topics to a level of debate that transcends the sole interests of the financial community.

Finally, an active and independent media needs to be cultivated—one that has the ability to raise critical issues about corporations and society. Two recent documentaries by independent filmmakers— Morgan Spurlock's *Supersize Me*, which raises issues about the health effects of the fast food industry, and *The Corporation*, by Mark Achbar, Jennifer Abbott, and Joel Bakan, which argues that the large corporation as currently conceived is fundamentally harmful to society—are examples of how informed and critical debate about corporations and society can be fostered through vehicles that span the gap between education, entertainment, and action. Government's role in preventing overconcentration in the media can be crucial in this regard.

Most fundamentally, increasing public discourse requires cultural change. In an era when corporations have broadened their roles in society, a corresponding broadening of discussions about how well they are playing these new roles is a necessity. Government, corporations, and individuals all need to consider carefully how this new and necessary level of discourse can best be achieved.

CHAPTER SEVEN

Government's Role
and the Road Ahead

TODAY, THE PIECES OF THE PUZZLE THAT SHOWS HOW TO CREATE markets that guide corporations toward the public interest are on the table, but they have yet to be sorted out and assembled. To make sure that power and influence are not turned over to corporations without a countervailing ability to direct them to the common good, change needs to be driven through a system that acts and reacts without fail. As we have seen, the three key components of this system are data, debate, and consequences—and government must play a critical role in ensuring the effectiveness of all three.

To construct a comprehensive system in which investors, consumers, and other stakeholders can be heard effectively, much effort and expense are necessary. But the rewards will be substantial: flexible and innovative solutions to the challenges of creating long-term wealth, a platform for informed and orderly debate, and an end to the distrust of corporations so widely felt today.

Government will need to ensure that the system works, but it will not need to dictate specific results. Government will draw a clear line limiting corporations' abilities to externalize costs, exhaust resources, and abuse stakeholders. Corporations will have well-defined parameters within which to exercise their ingenuity in effectively internalizing costs, assuring sustainability, and increasing the wealth of stakeholders, including stockowners. In this new world, corporations will be susceptible to strong influence from investors, consumers, and other stakeholders who will be able to express their preferences and purpose with relative ease through the financial, consumer, and labor markets.

Dangers of Maintaining the Status Quo

There are many obstacles to creating this system, but if these obstacles are not overcome the risks will be great.

One risk is that of simple inaction—inaction that will allow today's polarized attitudes toward corporations to persist. On the one side, the rich and successful ignore scandals and abuse and tout the virtues of a system that often squanders long-term wealth for the benefit of a few. On the other side, the disempowered are increasingly angry as they witness displays of ostentatious wealth in a world where many struggle in poverty and see environmental riches destroyed to satisfy the desires of cultures with little concern for the future. The world has seen all too often the dangers to which such highly polarized societies can lead.

The risks are equally great if only halfway measures are taken: for example, if there is just enough progress made on corporate social responsibility data and debate to hold out a promise of keeping corporations in line, but not enough to bring about real change. Or if there is just enough social and environmental information available to perceive the outline of a few companies' contributions to society, but not enough to understand the full implications of their acts or compare all companies meaningfully. Just enough consequences to reward and punish the exceptional few corporations, but not enough to do so consistently or predictably for the many. Just enough progress to quiet today's concerns, but not enough to head off another wave of scandals tomorrow.

Government Needs to Help

Disclosure of social and environmental data must be comprehensive and reliable, but it is unlikely that the marketplace and voluntary measures alone can ensure this kind of completeness today, tomorrow, and in the future. To ensure this disclosure government has a variety of regulatory and quasi-regulatory means at its disposal, such as requiring CSR disclosure in financial statements, imposing listing requirements for CSR information by stock exchanges,[1] changing accounting standards to require CSR reporting, mandating disclosure of disaggregated targeted data, requiring corporations that do business with governmental agencies to disclose CSR data, offering governmental certification programs for CSR disclosure, and creating governmental tax or regulatory incentives tied to CSR transparency. Whatever combination of mechanisms the government ultimately employs, the goal is the same: to compel the broad distribution of comprehensive data.

Analysis must be far-reaching and reliable, debate needs to be well informed and widespread, and understanding and concern about business needs to become part of everyday life. Government can play an essential role here as well. Funding research, particularly pure research, is a role that government assumes in many fields. It could easily do so in the fields of SRI and CSR. The public pension funds of cities, counties, and states have a public interest in ensuring that reliable analysis is available to guide their investment processes toward the public good. Regulators that require disclosure of specialized social and environmental data could make commitments to having that data easily accessible, widely distributed, and reliably analyzed. Government purchasing agencies at all levels that have preferential purchasing programs could fund sound analyses on which to base their decisions.

Government can also improve the system's chances of success by judiciously enhancing the power of stakeholders to communicate with and influence management. There is a fine line here between ensuring that an isolated management does not impose unacceptable costs on stockowners, stakeholders, or society and protecting concerned management from unreasonable demands. Filtering stakeholder communications through boards of directors is one possibility for a controlled approach. To do this, corporate boards of directors will have to develop an expertise that bears on the public interest, as well as on stock price or profits. Empowering stakeholders to intervene at limited crucial points in business decision making, such as during mergers and acquisitions, could also prove effective. There is much that government could also do to ensure that CSR data and analysis about corporations are available by giving consumers increased access to data and analysis at the point of purchase, whether through labeling, certification, or other means, and by ensuring retail investors easy access to CSR data in their stock picking. Governments at all levels can send powerful messages and encourage broad debate through their own roles as consumers and investors as well.

Government must keep its own workings free of undue influence by the business community if it is to encourage these developments and maintain a system that ensures an honest and transparent marketplace. It is no less true in our day than it was in that of Adam Smith that the voice of the business community should be treated with "suspicious attention" in the political arena. A system in which business is perceived to have had too great a hand in setting the ground rules will lack the legitimacy needed to establish trust or consensus in society.

A Cultural Shift Is Needed

No government initiative will have meaning, however, unless investors, consumers, employees, communities, and corporations themselves become involved. Unfortunately, today's culture tends to drive investors to pursue blindly the highest short-term returns and consumers to demand products always at the lowest price. For these instincts to change, individuals must think differently and interact with corporations in new ways—as consumers, investors, and employees. Just as corporations have multiple stakeholders, so individuals are stakeholders in multiple corporations, and as such they have many opportunities to take responsible action.

How members of society determine what to do with their financial assets—as individuals, as investors, and as consumers—can change. Individuals can come to understand the full stories of the banks with which they do daily business and choose carefully where to allocate their resources. Investors can come to understand the social and environmental philosophies and expertise of those to whom they entrust their assets and ensure their own beliefs are adequately represented in the financial marketplace. Consumers can come to understand the story of long-term wealth creation or destruction that lies behind the products and services they purchase every day and let this knowledge inform their choices. Employees can consider the social and environmental implications of where and how their employers conduct their business and can advocate needed change in the workplace, or when in the job market, can seek out employers who best mirror their concerns.

It is the responsibility not only of investors, consumers, employees, and the business world to participate actively but of schools and academia, the news and entertainment industries, and public service organizations to make ongoing debate more compelling, more widespread, and easier.

It is incumbent upon individuals and upon corporations themselves to demand that such a system be created. Although it is true that government's role in creating a reliable system is crucial, until investors, consumers, and other corporate stakeholders make it clear that they need data, debate, and consequences and will put them to good use, regulators are unlikely to take serious initiatives.

There are several reasons why corporations themselves should lobby for this new system. To begin with, if corporate abuse of new-found freedoms goes unchecked, the public may become so disillusioned that it will demand a return to more direct government control. In addition, a system that encourages stakeholders to communicate on issues of broad societal concern will provide corporate management with guidance on often controversial social issues. Finally, although corporations have been protected in the past from having to compete with their peers on social and environmental factors, those days are gone. The effects of corporations on society and the environment today are too important to ignore.

A Critical Need, Lasting Success

It is crucial that this kind of system be put in place soon. Without it, societies around the world will not have the tools they need to calculate the successes and failures of the movement of the past three decades away from government and toward market economies. Much power has been handed to the corporate world without much accountability, without clear goals or expectations of what constitutes success. If the gamble on corporations and the marketplace that many governments have made proves ill-advised or only partly successful, these tools will allow governments to take the actions needed to restore proper balance in an orderly fashion.

Among those gains that societies can look forward to in a world where this kind of market-based system, maintained by watchful government, has achieved success will be a new diversity and variety in ways of thinking. Individuals will think of themselves as stakeholders with a stake in multiple corporations. They will absorb much more information about these corporations, their characters and everyday actions, and will consciously express their responses through their daily banking, consuming, and investing. They will look beyond price and returns to consider the wealth that corporations create that will last beyond immediate profits. They will assess and comprehend the variety of forms that wealth can take, and learn to value it when they see it in their daily lives.

The corporate world itself will become more varied in its approaches to wealth creation. Its story will no longer be one of simple price. Small and local businesses will display their values close to home. Global corporations will make their case for wealth created around the world. Whether big or small, each corporation will choose to concentrate on a wealth that may include quality, sustainability, care for employees, or strengthening of community—each in its own way and according to its individual character. Some will devote exceptional resources to empowering and educating employees, others will find innovative means of enriching and enhancing the environment, others will take providing access to capital to those in need as their central goal. With each specialized effort, entrepreneurs will put the freedom of their imaginations to work to solve problems old and new. In this world, fully informed investors, consumers, and employees will have the opportunity to support those solutions that create wealth that builds a long-lasting society and shun those that do not.

Distinctions between socially responsible investing and the mainstream financial world will blur, as will the lines between corporate social responsibility and the responsible management of a firm. The emphasis will be on the responsibility of stakeholders to the corporation, as much as on the responsibilities of the corporation to its stakeholders. Corporate managers and their stakeholders will share a long-term view of the goals of the enterprise, their responsibilities to each other, and their relationship to others in society. Business will be more a part of daily life, and conversely, daily life will be more a part of business. The government will draw clear lines beyond which corporations cannot operate, distinguish clearly which goods should be provided by the public sphere and which goods private enterprise should provide, and ensure that corporations do not abuse the rules of the game.

In sum, the changed world that I envision will require more work, more awareness, and more decision making, but with that effort will come the knowledge that the wealth that is being created will last for generations to come.

Notes

Web sites cited in these notes were last visited in October 2004, unless otherwise noted.

Preface

1 See Sandra Waddock, "Parallel Universes: Companies, Academics, and the Progress of Corporate Citizenship," *Business and Society Review,* 2004, *109*(1), 5–42.

2 Steven D. Lydenberg, Alice Tepper Marlin, Sean O'Brien Strub, and the Council on Economic Priorities, *Rating America's Corporate Conscience: A Provocative Guide to the Companies Behind the Products You Buy Every Day* (Reading, Mass.: Addison-Wesley, 1986).

3 Peter Kinder, Steven D. Lydenberg, and Amy L. Domini (eds.), *The Social Investment Almanac: A Comprehensive Guide to Socially Responsible Investing* (New York: Henry Holt, 1992); Peter Kinder, Steven D. Lydenberg, and Amy L. Domini, *Investing for Good: Making Money While Being Socially Responsible* (New York: HarperBusiness, 1993).

4 Social Investment Forum, *2003 Report on Socially Responsible Investing Trends in the United States* (Washington, D.C.: Social Investment Forum, 2003), ii.

5 For an excellent history of the early days of shareholder activism in the United States, see David Vogel, *Lobbying the Corporation* (New York: Basic Books, 1978).

6 For an account of social entrepreneurship in action, see David Bornstein, *How to Change the World: Social Entrepreneurs and the Power of New Ideas* (Oxford, England: Oxford University Press, 2004).

7 For example, Sweden's AP1 Fund, with approximately $12 billion in assets, screens its assets according to international treaties and norms on human rights, labor, the environment, bribery, corruption, and the use of certain weapons. Its assessments are based on research provided by GES Investment Services. For a description of the fund's screens, see its Web site at: http://www.ap1.se/templates/AP1_Normal.asp?id=2368.

8 "Huge French Fund Applies SRI to €3 Billion of Its Assets," *Ethical Performance,* May 2004, 6(1). Available to subscribers at: http://www.ethicalperformance.com/subscribers/articles/pages/0601504/08.html.

9 See the JSE Securities Exchange press release, "Launch of JSE Socially Responsible Investment Index," May 19, 2004. Available at: www.jse.co.za/news/sri_launch.doc.

10 See the United Nations Global Compact Web site at: http://www.unglobalcompact
.org/Portal/Default.asp.
11 Steven D. Lydenberg, "Envisioning Socially Responsible Investing: A Model for 2006,"
Journal of Corporate Citizenship, Autumn 2002, 7, 57–77; and Steven D. Lydenberg, "Trust
Building and Trust Busting: Corporations, Government and Responsibilities," *Journal of
Corporate Citizenship*, Autumn 2003, *11*, 23–27.

Chapter One

1 Among the sources I found particularly helpful for this section were Jeff Gates, *Democracy
at Risk: Rescuing Main Street from Wall Street* (Cambridge, Mass.: Perseus Publishing, 2000);
David C. Korten, *When Corporations Rule the World* (San Francisco: Berrett-Koehler, 2001);
John Micklethwait and Adrian Wooldridge, *The Company: A Short History of a Revolutionary
Idea* (New York: Modern Library, 2003); Jerry Z. Muller, *The Mind and the Market: Capital-
ism in Modern European Thought* (New York: Knopf, 2002); Raghuram G. Rajan and Luigi
Zingales, *Saving Capitalism from the Capitalists: Unleashing the Power of Financial Markets to
Create Wealth and Spread Prosperity* (New York: Crown Business, 2003). Interested readers
may see also Russell Sparkes, "From Mortmain to Adam Smith: Historical Insights on the
Problem of Corporate Social Responsibility," in José Allouche (ed.), *The Development of the
Idea of Corporate Social Responsibility* (Adelaide, Australia: European Foundation for Management Development, forthcoming).
2 Micklethwait and Wooldridge, *The Company*, pp. 24–28.
3 As cited in Ethan B. Kapstein, "Distributive Justice as an International Public Good: A
Historical Perspective," in Inge Kaul, Isabelle Grunberg, and Marc A. Stern (eds.), *Global
Public Goods: International Cooperation in the 21st Century* (Oxford, England: Oxford University Press, 1999), 94.
4 Kapstein, "Distributive Justice," p. 93.
5 William Greider, *The Soul of Capitalism: Opening Paths to a Moral Economy* (New York: Simon
& Schuster, 2003), 38.
6 David Wessel, "A Lesson from the Blackout: Free Markets Also Need Rules," *Wall Street
Journal*, August 28, 2003, p. A1.
7 Adam Smith, *The Wealth of Nations* (New York: Modern Library, 2000), 484-5.
8 Smith, *Wealth of Nations*, pp. 747–790. Smith saw the government's duties to include
national defense, a system of justice, and certain public works that were too expensive for
private enterprise to profit from, such as building and maintaining roads, bridges, harbors,
and forts.
9 See Muller, *The Mind and the Market*, pp. 76–80, for more on Adam Smith's view of the visible hand of government.
10 Smith, *Wealth of Nations*, p. 288.

Chapter Two

1   See John Elkington, *Cannibals with Forks: The Triple Bottom Line of 21st-Century Business* (Gabriola Island, British Columbia: New Society Publishers, 1998); Paul Hawken, Amory Lovins, and L. Hunter Lovins, *Natural Capitalism: Creating the Next Industrial Revolution* (Boston: Little Brown, 1999); Jane Jacobs, *The Nature of Economies* (New York: Random House, 2000); Margaret Blair, *Ownership and Control: Rethinking Corporate Governance for the Twenty-First Century* (Washington, D.C.: Brookings Institution, 1995); Marcy Murninghan, "Common Sense and Civic Virtue: Institutional Investors, Responsible Ownership, and the Democratic Ideal," *New England Journal of Public Policy, 18*(2), 83–146; Don Tapscott and David Ticoll, *The Naked Corporation: How the Age of Transparency Will Revolutionize Business* (New York: Free Press, 2003); Bornstein, *How to Change the World*; Stephen Young, *Moral Capitalism: Reconciling Private Interest with the Public Good* (San Francisco: Berrett-Koehler, 2003); William Greider, *The Soul of Capitalism: Opening Paths to a Moral Economy* (New York: Simon & Schuster, 2003); Jed Emerson and Sheila Bonini, *The Blended Value Map: Tracking the Intersects and Opportunities of Economic, Social, and Environmental Value Creation* (paper), October 2003, available on the Web site of Blendedvalue.org at: http://www .blendedvalue.org/Papers/default.aspx.

2   See Jon P. Gunneman, "Capital Ideas: Theology Engages the Economic," *Religion and Values in Public Life* (journal of Harvard Divinity School), 7(1), 5–8.

3   See Amartya Sen, *Development as Freedom* (New York: Anchor Books, 1999) for a discussion of freedom as an instrument for, and the result of, successful development.

4   The information presented on the following five companies was obtained from their Web sites and from correspondence and conversations with their staff. Similarly, details on companies and organizations profiled later in this book were generally obtained from information available on their Web sites and from correspondence and conversations with their staff.

5   Jack Stack, *The Great Game of Business* (New York: Doubleday, 1992).

6   Ira A. Jackson and Jane Nelson, *Profits with Principles: Seven Strategies for Delivering Value with Values* (New York: Doubleday, 2004).

7   James C. Collins and Jerry I. Porras, "Building Your Company Vision," *Harvard Business Review*, September-October 1996, p. 67.

8   For an excellent overview of the topic of public goods in an international context, see Kaul, Grunberg, and Stern, *Global Public Goods*.

9   See P. W. Singer, *Corporate Warriors: The Rise of the Privatized Military Industry* (Ithaca, N.Y.: Cornell University Press, 2003) for a fascinating account of the recent rise of private military forces.

Chapter Three

1   See the World Business Council on Sustainable Development's Web site at: http://www .wbcsd.ch.

2   For an excellent statement of the case for the values-driven model of corporate social responsibility, see the Forum for the Future and British Telecom, *Just Values: Beyond the Business Case for Sustainable Development* (2003). Occasional paper available at: http://www .forumforthefuture.org.uk/publications/JustValuesPublication_page760.aspx.

3   See Green Mountain Coffee Roasters' press release, "Green Mountain Coffee Hires Director of Social Responsibility," *Business Wire*, March 20, 2001. Contact *Business Wire* at http://www.businesswire.com.

4   Chris Reidy, "Boots Laced with Beliefs," *Boston Globe*, August 8, 2000, p. G1.

5   Johnson & Johnson's home page contains a link to its Credo. See: http://www.jnj.com/ our_company/our_credo/index.htm.

6   See Enron's 2000 annual report, available at: www.enron.com/corp/investors/annuals/ 2000/ourvalues.html.

7   See ISO press release 924, "ISO to Go Ahead with Guidelines for Social Responsibility," June 29, 2004. Available at: www.iso.org/iso/en/commcentre/pressreleases/2004/ Ref924.html.

8   See Pi Environmental Consulting and Pacific Institute, *Certification and Trade Policy Strategic Assessment* (white paper prepared for the ISEAL Alliance), February 2004. Available on the ISEAL Web site at: http://www.isealalliance.org/documents/index.htm#technical.

9   Two recent books that serve as guides to corporate codes of conduct are Deborah Leipziger, *The Corporate Responsibility Code Book* (Sheffield, U.K.: Greenleaf Publishing, 2003), and S. Prakash Sethi, *Setting Global Standards: Guidelines for Creating Codes of Conduct in Multinational Corporations* (New York: Wiley, 2003).

10 James E. Post, Lee E. Preston, and Sybille Sachs, *Redefining the Corporation: Stakeholder Management and Organizational Wealth* (Stanford, Calif.: Stanford Business Books, 2002), 53.

Chapter Four

1   Council on Economic Priorities, *Shortchanged: Minorities and Women in Banking* (Economic Priorities Report), September-October 1972, 3(4), 7.

2   See the Corporate Register Web site at: http://www.corporateregister.com/charts/ charts.pl.

3   See CSRwire's Web site at: http://www.csrwire.com/csr/home.mpl. The Web site also contains a CSR directory with links to approximately a thousand organizations around the world working on CSR issues.

4   Muller, *The Mind and the Market*, pp. 364–366.

5   Global Reporting Initiative, *Sustainability Reporting Guidelines*, 2002. Available at: http://www.globalreporting.org/guidelines/2002.asp.

6   See the GRI reports database on its Web site at: http://www.globalreporting.org/ guidelines/reports/search.asp; accessed September 2004. GRI regularly updates the number of companies.

7   See the GRI Web site at: http://www.globalreporting.org/guidelines/reporters_IA.asp; accessed September 2004.

8   See Utopies, *Etat du reporting sur développement durable, 2003*. Available from Utopies, 53 rue de Turenne, 75003 Paris, France. See also the presentation "Impact of the French Law on Mandatory Reporting: Key Results of the Utopies/UNEP/SustainAbility 2003 Benchmarking Survey," by Stan Dupré, April 21, 2004, on the Institute for Responsible Investment Web site at: http://www.bc.edu/centers/ccc/Media/utopies.pdf.

9   See *The Operating and Financial Review: Practical Guidance for Directors*, available at: http://www.dti.gov.uk/cld/pdfs/ofr_guide.pdf. For a more general discussion of proposed regulations relating to the OFR, see a description of the draft regulations issued in May 2004 at: http://www.dti.gov.uk/cld/financialreview.htm.

10 U.S. Securities and Exchange Commission, Release No. 33-51870, July 19, 1971.

11 *Environmental Disclosure: SEC Should Explore Ways to Improve Tracking and Transparency of Information* (Report No. GAO-04-808). (Washington, D.C.: Government Accountability Office, July 2004), 4.

12 See Sanford Lewis and Tim Little, *Fooling Investors & Fooling Themselves: How Aggressive Corporate Accounting & Asset Management Tactics Can Lead to Environmental Accounting Fraud* (Oakland, Calif.: Rose Foundation, 2004), and Susan Blake Goodman and Tim Little, *The Gap in GAAP: An Examination of Environmental Accounting Loopholes* (Oakland, Calif.: Rose Foundation, 2003). Both studies are available on the foundation's Web site at: http://www.rosefdn.org/efp.html. Also see SEC Petition No. 4-463, September 20, 2002, available at: http://www.rosefdn.org/images/SEC_Enviro_Disclosure_Pet.pdf.

13 See the Corporate Sunshine Working Group Web site at: http://www.corporatesunshine.org/proposedisclosure.pdf.

14 Cynthia A. Williams, "The Securities and Exchange Commission and Corporate Social Transparency," *Harvard Law Review*, 1998–99, *112*, 1204.

15 See the Web site at: www.facilityreporting.org.

16 See "What Is the Toxics Release Inventory (TRI) Program?" on the EPA's Web site at: http://www.epa.gov/tri/whatis.htm.

17 See the EPA's Web site at: www.epa.gov/tri/programs/other_federal.htm.

18 See Suncor Energy, *What's at Stake? 2003 Report on Sustainability*. Available at: http://www.suncor.com/data/1/rec_docs/25_SuncorSDReport2003.pdf.

19 See Dofasco, Inc., *2002 Annual Report*, pp. 22–27. Available at: http://www.dofasco.ca/INVESTORS/annual_report/env_energy_2.htm.

20 See Baxter International, *2002 Sustainability Report: Our Progress* (Deerfield, Ill.: Baxter International), 50.

21 See the Body Shop's Web site at: www.thebodyshopinternational.com/web/tbsgl/reporting_approach.jsp#1.

Chapter Five

1   I would like to thank Professor Joshua Margolis of the Harvard Business School for point-
    ing out this particularly apt term to me.

2   See RTK Net's Web site at: http://www.rtknet.org. For details on use of its information,
    see Alain MacLean, *The Right Stuff: Information in the Public Interest* (Washington, D.C.:
    RTK Net, 1995). Available at: http://www.rtknet.org/reports/rightstuff.html.

3   See Nicholas Zamiska, "Judge Orders OSHA to Release Safety Data for U.S. Companies,"
    Wall Street Journal, August 4, 2004, p. D2.

4   See the Web site at: http://www.business-humanrights.org.

5   Number of strengths and concerns reflects the ratings of companies as of July 2004; rat-
    ings may have changed since. Available on the *Socrates* database at: http://web.kld.com/
    socrates.

6   See note 5.

7   See Innovest, *Intangible Value Assessment: Alcan, Inc.*, September 2002, p. 1. Available on
    Innnovest's Web site at: http://www.innovestgroup.com.

8   See Innovest, "The U.S. Electric Utility Industry: Uncovering Hidden Value Potential for
    Strategic Investors," June 2002, pp. 7–9. Available on Innovest's Web site at: http://www
    .innovestgroup.com.

9   See the sample Intangible Value Assessment profile of Alcan, Inc., posted on Innovest's
    Web site at: http://www.innovestgroup.com.

10 "Rating Agencies Will Submit to New Standard," *Ethical Performance*, April 2004, 5(11).
    Available to subscribers at: http://www.ethicalperformance.com/subscribers/articles/
    pages05110404/12.html.

11 It should be noted that employee-owned companies, like other companies, can have prob-
    lems. For example, UAL, the employee-owned parent of United Airlines, faced severe
    financial difficulties in 2004. YSI discusses in its CERES report its dealings with the com-
    munity of Yellow Springs in relation to wells on and near its property with solvent-related
    contaminants.

12 See Investors' Circle Web site at: http://www.investorscircle.net/social%20responsibility
    .html.

13 For a description of REDF's experience with social return on investment, see Cynthia
    Gair, "A Report from the Good Ship SROI." Available on the REDF Web site at:
    http://www.redf.org/about_sroi.htm.

14 Emerson and Bonini, *The Blended Value Map*.

15 Jed Emerson, Timothy Freundlich, and Shari Berenbach, "The Investor's Toolkit: Gener-
    ating Multiple Returns Through a Unified Investment Strategy (white paper), summer
    2004, p. 12. Available at: http://www.blendedvalue.org/Additional+Papers+by+Jed+
    Emerson/default.aspx.

16 Bill McKibben, "Small World: Why One Town Stays Unplugged," *Harper's*, December
    2003, p. 54.

17 For an excellent discussion of sustainable agriculture and price, see Frances Moore Lappé and Anna Lappé, *Hope's Edge: The Next Diet for a Small Planet* (New York: Tarcher/Putnam, 2002). See p. 222 on "seeing price differently" and p. 266 on "the real cost of food."

18 Sandra Waddock, *Leading Corporate Citizens: Vision, Values, Value Added* (New York: McGraw-Hill/Irwin, 2002), 5.

19 "100 Best Corporate Citizens for 2004," *Business Ethics*, 2004, 18(1), pp. 8–12.

20 Presentation by Thomas Linzey, staff attorney for CELDF at the Tellus Institute, March 16, 2004. See also the CELDF Web site at: http://www.celdf.org. In particular, see the model brief to eliminate corporate rights at: http://www.ratical.org/corporations/demoBrief.html.

Chapter Six

1 James Hawley and Andrew Williams, *The Rise of Fiduciary Capitalism: How Institutional Investors Can Make Corporate America More Democratic* (Philadelphia: University of Pennsylvania Press, 2000).

2 See the Web site of the Interfaith Center on Corporate Responsibility for a listing of shareholder resolutions on social and environmental issues filed for the 2004 season at: http://www.iccr.org/shareholder/proxy_book04/04statuschart.php.

3 See the Domini Social Investments press release, "Advocacy Groups and Shareholders Persuade Procter & Gamble to Offer Fair Trade Coffee," September 15, 2003. Available at: http://www.domini.com/about-domini/News/Press-Release-Archive/.

4 See the Carbon Disclosure Project's Web site at: http://www.cdproject.net/about.asp.

5 See the Publish What You Pay Web site at: http://www.publishwhatyoupay.org/eiti/.

6 See the CERES press release, "Thirteen Pension Leaders Call on SEC Chairman to Require Global Warming Risks in Corporate Disclosure," April 15, 2004. Available at: http://ceres.org/newsroom/press/invest_sec_disclosure.htm.

7 Robert Monks and Allen Sykes, *Capitalism Without Owners Will Fail: A Policymaker's Guide to Reform* (London: Centre for the Study of Financial Innovation, 2002), 36.

8 U.S. Securities and Exchange Commission, Release No. 34-48626, IC-26206, October 14, 2003.

9 Lappé and Lappé, *Hope's Edge*, p. 112.

10 See the Grameen Bank Web site at: http://www.grameen-info.org/bank/GBGlance.htm.

11 See the Accion International Web site at: http://www.accion.org/about_key_stats.asp.

12 See the Women's World Banking Web site at: http://www.swwb.org/English/1000/our_impact.htm.

13 Social Investment Forum, *2003 Report on Socially Responsible Investing Trends in the United States*, 24.

14 CDFI Fund press release, "$17 Million Awarded to Banks & Thrifts for Work in Distressed Communities," July 12, 2004. Available at: http://www.cdfifund.gov/news/2004/2004BEAawards.pdf.

15 National Federation of Community Development Credit Unions press release, "Federation Launches New Grant Programs: RFPs Promote Partnership, Fight Payday Lending," June 21, 2004. Available at: http://www.natfed.org/i4a/pages/index.cfm?pageid=766.

16 See the Commons Capital Web site at: http://www.commonscapital.com/htm/portfolio .htm.

17 See Boston Community Capital, 2002–2003 Annual Report, pp. 4, 15. Available from Boston Community Capital at: http://www.bostoncommunitycapital.org.

18 See the RISE Web site at: http://www.riseproject.org.

19 Social Investment Forum, 2003 Report on Socially Responsible Investing Trends in the United States, ii, 9.

20 See Peter Camejo, The SRI Advantage: Why Socially Responsible Investing Has Outperformed Financially (Gabriola Island, British Columbia: New Society Publishers, 2002).

21 For those interested in the academic literature on this debate, a Web site maintained by Lloyd Kurtz contains an extensive annotated bibliography and a selection of sixteen highly pertinent articles; see sristudies.org. The Social Investment Forum's 2003 Socially Responsible Investing Trends in the United States report also lists a number of studies published between 2001 and 2003 on both SRI fund performance and company and stock performance; see pp. 47–49.

22 Meir Statman, "Socially Responsible Mutual Funds," Financial Analysts Journal, May-June 2000, 56(3), 30–39.

23 Joshua Daniel Margolis and James Patrick Walsh, People and Profits? The Search for a Link Between a Company's Social and Financial Performance (Hillsdale, N.J.: Erlbaum, 2001), 10–11.

24 See Casio's 2003 Environmental Report at: world.casio.com/env/pdf/report_2003/ p23.pdf.

25 See KLD Research & Analytics' Socrates database profiles of General Motors and Hewlett-Packard. Available at: http://web.kld.com/socrates; accessed July 2004.

26 See the U.S. Environmental Protection Agency Web site at: http://www.epa.gov/oppt/ epp/about/faq.htm#General/Background%20Questions.

27 Raymond Leung, "Greening of Supply Chain Management," International Green Productivity Association Newsletter, September 2003, 5(3). Available at: http://igpa.ema.org.tw/ newsletter/2003n003/2003n0030103.htm.

28 Dr. Ning Yu, "Green Procurement in the Republic of China on Taiwan," International Green Productivity Association Newsletter, September 2003, 5(3). Available at: http://igpa.ema.org .tw/newsletter/2003n003/2003n0030201.htm.

29 2003 Report on Fair Trade Trends in the U.S., Canada & the Pacific Rim (Washington, D.C.: Fair Trade Federation, 2003), 1. Available at: http://www.fairtradefederation.com/2003_ trends_report.pdf.

30 See the European Fair Trade Association Web site at: http://www.eftafairtrade.org/efta .asp.

31 Michael Paulson, "Fair-Market Coffee Firm Reaches Deal with Church," Boston Globe, November 29, 2003, p. B1.

32 Stephen Davis, "U.S. Reform Will Spark Industry Revolution," *Financial Times*, June 21, 2004, p. FTFM 7.

33 Available on Merrill Lynch's Web site at: http://www.mlim.ml.com/USA/template.asp? nav_id=IndInvestors&RURL=/content/Retail/html/proxyvotingpolicies.htm&MB=x.

34 Available on AIM Investments' Web site at: http://www.aiminvestments.com/generic/ 0,,-1_15605.htm#2.

35 See Ian McDonald, "Ten Fund Firms' Proxy Votes on Pay Reflect Urging of Unions," *Wall Street Journal*, September 3, 2004, p. C3. For a compilation of a number of mutual fund proxy voting guidelines, see Daniel T. Larner, "Mutual Fund Proxy-Voting Guidelines: New Opportunities to Promote Socially Responsible Proxy Voting," unpublished research paper (Washington, D.C.: Social Investment Forum, February 2004). Also see Beth Healy, "Mutual Fund Votes Show Limits to Change," *Boston Globe*, September 5, 2004, p. A1. The Social Investment Forum will issue a report in 2004 reviewing the proxy voting records of the top ten U.S. mutual funds on social and environmental issues.

36 See Ontario Securities Commission, *Proposed National Instrument 81-106 Investment Fund Continuous Disclosure, Part 10, Notice and Request for Comment*, May 28, 2004. Available at: http://www.osc.gov.on.ca/Regulation/Rulemaking/Current/Part8/rule_20040528_81 -106_pro-ni-ifcd.jsp.

37 *Delegating Shareholder Engagement, Local Authority Pension Funds and Fund Managers: A Survey of Policy and Practice* (Bradford, United Kingdom: Local Authority Pension Fund Forum, July 2004), 3–4.

38 Albert O. Hirschman, *Exit, Voice, and Loyalty: Responses to Decline in Firms, Organizations, and States* (Cambridge, Mass.: Harvard University Press, 1970), 117.

39 See Verité's *Emerging Markets Research Report, Year-End Report*, November, 2003. Available at: http://www.calpers.ca.gov/eip-docs/about/press/news/invest-corp/verite-report -2003.pdf.

40 Wilshire Associates, *Permissible Equity Markets Investment Analysis*, February 2004, pp. 11–15. Available at: http://www.calpers.ca.gov/eip-docs/about/press/news/invest-corp/ 2004-perm-eqty-als.pdf.

41 See the Sam Group's Web site at: http://www.sam-group.com/htmle/research/ methodology/value.cfm.

42 See "FTSE4Good Index Series: Inclusion Criteria" available on the FTSE Web site at: http://www.ftse.com/ftse4good/index.jsp.

Chapter Seven

1 In mid-2004, the London Stock Exchange announced that it would create a "corporate responsibility exchange" for data on the social and environmental performance of companies listed on the exchange. See "LSE Sets Up Data Repository," *Ethical Performance*, September 2004, 6(4). Available to subscribers at: http//www.ethicalperformance.com// subscribers/articles/pages/06040904/09.html. See also the London Stock Exchange web site at: http://www.londonstockexchange.com/en-gb/products/irs/cre/.

Index

About the Author

STEVEN LYDENBERG HAS SPENT THIRTY YEARS IN THE SOCIAL investment and corporate social accountability worlds. From 1975 to 1987, he conducted research on issues of corporate social accountability for the Council on Economic Priorities (CEP). There he authored studies of the role of corporate financing in the political process, the filing of shareholder resolutions, and corporate initiatives in the areas of dependent care and minority banking. As director of corporate accountability research at CEP, he was coauthor, along with Alice Tepper Marlin and Sean O'Brien Strub, of *Rating America's Corporate Conscience*, published in 1986. This book provided the first systematic ratings of the corporate social accountability records of major U.S. corporations for a consumer audience. In 1987, he joined Franklin Research and Development Corporation (now Trillium Asset Management), where he worked as an investment analyst, contributing to the company's *Insight* newsletter. Franklin Research was the first U.S. money management firm to specialize exclusively in serving socially responsible investors.

In 1990, with Amy Domini and Peter Kinder, he cofounded Kinder, Lydenberg, Domini & Co. (now KLD Research & Analytics, Inc.), where he served for eleven years as research director. During that time he helped create and maintain the Domini Social Index, the first socially screened equity index in the United States. He also played a key role in developing the company's *Socrates* database, a major resource for KLD clients. With his partners he coedited *The Social Investment Almanac* (1992) and coauthored *Investing for Good* (1993). More recently, his articles "Envisioning Socially Responsible Investing: A Model for 2006" and "Trust Building and Trust Busting: Corporations, Government, and Responsibilities" appeared in the *Journal of Corporate Citizenship* in 2002 and 2003, respectively.

Today Lydenberg is chief investment officer for Domini Social Investments LLC and director of the Institute for Responsible Investment at the Center for Corporate Citizenship at Boston College. In 2001 he received the First Affirmative Financial Network SRI Service Award for outstanding contributions to the SRI community. He has also served on numerous advisory boards and judging panels, including those for the Business Ethics Magazine Business Ethics Awards, Social Accountability International's Corporate Conscience Awards, the CERES-ACCA Awards for Sustainable Reporting, and Leeds School of Business Summit Award for Social Impact.

Lydenberg earned his bachelor of arts degree in English from Columbia College and a master of fine arts degree from Cornell University. In 1990 the CFA Institute designated him a Chartered Financial Analyst (CFA).

Berrett-Koehler Publishers

B errett-Koehler is an independent publisher of books and other publications at the leading edge of new thinking and innovative practice on work, business, management, leadership, stewardship, career development, human resources, entrepreneurship, and global sustainability.

Since the company's founding in 1992, we have been committed to creating a world that works for all by publishing books that help us to integrate our values with our work and work lives, and to create more humane and effective organizations.

We have chosen to focus on the areas of work, business, and organizations, because these are central elements in many people's lives today. Furthermore, the work world is going through tumultuous changes, from the decline of job security to the rise of new structures for organizing people and work. We believe that change is needed at all levels—individual, organizational, community, and global—and our publications address each of these levels.

To find out about our new books,
special offers,
free excerpts,
and much more,
subscribe to our free monthly eNewsletter at

www.bkconnection.com

Please see next pages for other books
from Berrett-Koehler Publishers

More books from Berrett-Koehler Publishers

634

Alternatives to Economic Globalization
A Better World Is Possible, Second Edition

A Report of the International Forum
on Globalization

Written by a premier group of 21 thinkers from
around the world, the second edition of
Alternatives to Economic Globalization lays out
democratic, ecologically sound, socially just alternatives to corporate globalization more fully,
specifically, and thoughtfully than has ever been
done before.

Paperback, 312 pages • ISBN 1-57675-303-4 • Item #53034 $18.95

The People's Business
Controlling Corporations and Restoring
Democracy

Lee Drutman and Charlie Cray

The People's Business examines the growing
threat of unaccountable corporate power in our
society. Prompted by the collapse of Enron and
other cases of corporate crime, fraud and abuse,
The People's Business brings together the
thinking of many leading scholars and activists.
The result is a clear-headed plan of action to
restore citizen control over corporations.

Hardcover, 300 pages • ISBN 1-57675-309-3 • Item #53093 $24.95

Moral Capitalism
Reconciling Private Interest with the Public
Good

Stephen Young

Moral Capitalism is a handbook to the Caux
Roundtable's code of corporate ethics—which
has received attention around the world—
showing readers how to manage market
capitalism and globalization for economic and
social justice and fairness and how to improve
outcomes for people and societies from market
capitalism and globalization.

Hardcover, 235 pages • ISBN 1-57675-257-7 • Item #52577 $29.95

Berrett-Koehler Publishers
PO Box 565, Williston, VT 05495-9900
Call toll-free! **800-929-2929** 7 am-9 pm EST
Or fax your order to 1-802-864-7626
For fastest service order online: **www.bkconnection.com**

634

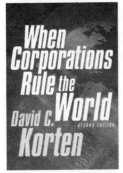

When Corporations Rule the World

Second Edition—Revised and Expanded, with five new chapters

David Korten offers an alarming exposé of the devastating consequences of economic globalization and a passionate message of hope in this well-reasoned, extensively researched analysis. He documents the human and environmental consequences of economic globalization, and explains why human survival depends on a community-based, people-centered alternative.

Paperback, 400 pages • ISBN 1-887208-04-6 • Item #08046 $16.95

Gangs of America
The Rise of Corporate Power and the Disabling of Democracy

Ted Nace

Through fascinating stories populated by colorful personalities, *Gangs of America* details the rise of corporate power in America. Driven to answer the central question of how corporations got more rights than people, Ted Nace delves deep into the origins of this institution that has become a hallmark of the modern age. He synthesizes the latest research with a compelling historical narrative to tell the rich tale of the rise of corporate power in America.

Hardcover, 292 pages • ISBN 1-57675-260-7 • Item #52607 $24.95

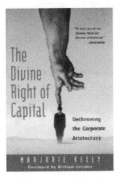

Divine Right of Capital
Dethroning the Corporate Aristocracy

Marjorie Kelly

In *The Divine Right of Capital*, Marjorie Kelly argues that focusing on the interests of stockholders to the exclusion of everyone else's interests is a form of discrimination based on property or wealth. She shows how this bias is held by our institutional structures, much as they once held biases against blacks and women. *The Divine Right of Capital* shows how to design more equitable alternatives—new property rights, new forms of corporate governance, new ways of looking at corporate performance—that build on both free-market and democratic principles.

Paperback, 290 pages • ISBN 1-57675-237-2 • Item #52372 $17.95
Hardcover, 290 pages • ISBN 1-57675-125-2 • Item #51252 $24.95

Berrett-Koehler Publishers
PO Box 565, Williston, VT 05495-9900
Call toll-free! **800-929-2929** 7 am-9 pm EST

Or fax your order to 1-802-864-7626
For fastest service order online: **www.bkconnection.com**

Spread the word!

Berrett-Koehler books are available at quantity discounts for orders of 10 or more copies.

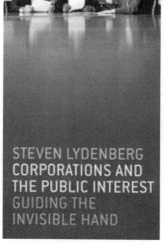

Corporations and the Public Interest

Guiding the Invisible Hand

Steven Lydenberg

Hardcover, 200 pages
ISBN 978-1-57675-291-3
Item #52913 $27.95

To find out about discounts for orders of 10 or more copies for individuals, corporations, institutions, and organizations, please call us toll-free at (800) 929-2929.

To find out about our discount programs for resellers, please contact our Special Sales department at (415) 288-0260; Fax: (415) 362-2512. Or email us at bkpub@bkpub.com.

Subscribe to our free e-newsletter!

To find out about what's happening at Berrett-Koehler and to receive announcements of our new books, special offers, free excerpts, and much more, subscribe to our free monthly e-newsletter at www.bkconnection.com.

Berrett-Koehler Publishers
PO Box 565, Williston, VT 05495-9900
Call toll-free! **800-929-2929** 7 am-9 pm EST

Or fax your order to 1-802-864-7626
For fastest service order online: **www.bkconnection.com**